About the Author

An experienced therapist, coach and trainer, Jenny lives in Oxfordshire with husband, Mike and Mollie the dog. She has a passion for working with women to help them overcome anxiety and depression, increase confidence and truly flourish.

Jenny has written extensively, including a period as resident therapist for *Top Santé* magazine, and author of two digital books for the academic and business market — *Overcoming Perfectionism* and *Managing Anxiety at Work* published by Bookboon.com.

Also, a seasoned broadcaster, Jenny was a regular guest and Agony Aunt for BBC Radio Oxford for fifteen years.

Email: jennygould3@binternet.com
Website: www.cbtoxford.co.uk
Facebook: https://www.facebook.com/jennygouldauthor
Twitter: @JenGouldAuthor

No More Good Girl
Overcome Anxiety, Dump the Guilt and Free Yourself

Jenny Gould

No More Good Girl
Overcome Anxiety, Dump the Guilt and Free Yourself

Olympia Publishers
London

www.olympiapublishers.com
OLYMPIA PAPERBACK EDITION

A CIP catalogue record for this title is
available from the British Library.

ISBN: 978-1-78830-934-9

First Published in 2021

Olympia Publishers
Tallis House
2 Tallis Street
London
EC4Y 0AB
Printed in Great Britain

Dedication

In memory of
Rosemary Trustam 1949 – 2020
Wise, principled and passionate
A true role model

Acknowledgements

The ideas in this book are a distillation of my own observations but, like all therapists, I owe a great deal to the learnings I have taken from a wealth of different sources, including the many books which have inspired me along the way. I'd just like to make special mention of my clinical supervisor, Dani Dennington who is a veritable fount of knowledge, which she shares from generously.

I'm very grateful to all colleagues, clients and friends with whom I've discussed my ideas for this book, especially those who helped by reading and commenting on earlier drafts. They are: Bernadette Simmons, Brigitte Malige, Chiron O'Keefe, Julia Thomas, Kathryn Payne, Lyn Kirby, Rachel White, Rosemary Trustam, Sharon Wallerson and Sue Bremner-Milne. Your encouragement was invaluable and without a doubt instrumental in keeping me on track.

Thanks to all the Good Girls I have known, who inspired me to want to make a difference, in particular my wonderful clients who have taught me so much about the human condition and what makes us tick.

Finally, thank you to Olympia Publishers for their expertise and help in getting this book out there to all those Good Girls. Without your interest in seeing the final manuscript I might never have finished it.

Disclaimer

Contents

Introduction

So why am I writing this book? As a therapist and coach, over the years I've worked with many clients struggling with this 'Good Girl' issue. What drove them to come for help was depression or anxiety (often both) or problems with their partner, family or work. What was contributing massively to all of this was that their Good Girl was in charge. During our work together, they learnt to take the steps needed to create positive change. Understanding themselves better, strengthening their self-belief and learning some effective techniques allowed them to break free from the grip of their Good Girl.

I write very much from personal experience too. As with most other Good Girls the problem began early on and was unconsciously reinforced as I went through life. I think it's true to say that I did have a somewhat difficult childhood. One Boxing Day when I was not yet five years old, and my sister a baby of six months, my father took his own life. In those days this kind of shame was something that would be swept under the carpet — a secret never to be talked about even within the family. In fact, I didn't find out the truth about what happened for many years.

My mother remarried eighteen months later and because my stepfather was in the army, it was the beginning of a new life, living first in the Far East and then Germany. Slowly his drinking spiralled out of control, and with that came more secrets and a very tangible feeling of shame — the constant companion of all children of alcoholics. But the overriding emotion was fear; waiting for Dad's unpredictable temper to explode, we never knew how things would be. My Mum spent much of her time trying to avoid making him angry, walking on eggshells to keep the peace. That was a horrible time.

By the age of fourteen I had been to fourteen different schools. I rarely stayed long enough to make firm friends and so always felt like an outsider. I tried hard to fit in, to be nice, to be friendly, but whatever I did to become accepted, it was never good enough. Then when I was 14, we were posted to Bahrain. That was the point at which they decided my education must come first and I was packed off to boarding school in Lyme Regis. I felt abandoned by my family and like an outsider at school. I hated it so much; if I ever get a whiff of apple blossom talcum powder, I'm transported straight back to that overpowering feeling of homesickness.

But slowly I began to fit in and find my feet, and in fact it turned out to be the best thing that could have happened. Being settled meant I developed real lasting friendships and for the first time perhaps, I felt accepted and mostly good enough. When I left, aged eighteen, my Good Girl was well disguised and although still very much part of me, I had become adept at making sure no one knew of my shame and vulnerability.

I'm pleased to report that these days my Good Girl is quieter and knows her place. However, there are definitely times when she intrudes, uninvited. I know she's around when I find myself avoiding a difficult conversation, feeling I've done something wrong or worrying that I've inadvertently upset someone.

So what about you? You may not have had a particularly difficult or unhappy childhood but somewhere along the way the foundations of good girl syndrome were insidiously put in place. My aim with this book is to lift the fog, share lots of tried and tested techniques and inspire you to push forward and change how you live your life.

Chapter 1
The Making of a Good Girl

'*When you say "yes" to others, make sure you aren't saying "no" to yourself.*' PAULO COELHO

I'm guessing that you worry too much about what others think, you're anxious about doing or saying the wrong thing and your greatest fear is that people won't like you. Am I right? Or perhaps you recognise yourself as a 'people pleaser', as someone who avoids conflict at all costs, but until now hadn't realised just how much your Good Girl might be running the show.

If this is you, I think you'll see a lot of yourself reflected in these pages.

What is Good Girl Syndrome?

It's a term used to describe those of us who seek approval; who are 'nice', helpful and dutiful, fear making mistakes or getting into trouble. We are Good Girls, but paradoxically we feel we are never good enough. Some of us are introvert and some extravert. Some of us drive ourselves onwards in the impossible quest for perfection, while others go through life avoiding, playing safe, or giving up on being the person they want to be. Either way, Good Girls live with self-doubt, shame, fear and anxiety. Think about these questions:

Do you hesitate to seek new opportunities, speak at meetings or give presentations? Does your fear of doing or saying the wrong thing hold you back?

Do you attract the wrong men? Are you inclined to go along with things to avoid conflict, unable to ask for what you want and need?

Do you do more than your share, feel taken advantage of? Always putting others' needs before your own? Do you push yourself to be the 'perfect' parent?

Does your fear of being judged prevent you from joining in and enjoying life? Has social media become a way of torturing yourself?

Are some of your friends too needy? Do you 'rescue' them but sometimes feel used and exhausted by it all?

If this is familiar to you, then your Good Girl has too much control over your life. But don't worry — the good news is you CAN learn to liberate yourself. I want to give you the tools to overcome fear, forget about guilt and stop living at the mercy of your emotions.

This is very much a 'how to' book. It will help you understand yourself better, but above all, give you the techniques to really begin thinking, feeling and behaving differently. Your confidence will grow and along with it a wonderful sense of freedom, as the real you, begins to emerge. Embracing and accepting yourself as the unique human being that you are allows you to fulfil your true potential and start creating the life you want.

Good Girls are everywhere. In fact, there are millions out there, and that includes me. These days I like to think of myself as somewhat liberated, though even as I write this, I realise I still have some way to go. I can't lie, I do find myself being drawn into old patterns, even now. But that's okay — old habits die hard, and my Good Girl has been with me for a very long time. For me progress was pretty slow because I didn't know how to change, not really. But, if you recognise yourself in this book (as I suspect you will), I hope you will be inspired to take action without further ado, and to make those changes, beginning right now.

On the face of it, it seems that the young women of today are much more confident and more assertive than their mothers and grandmothers, so why would they need to be even more so? The truth is that deep down many are still driven by an overwhelming need to be liked; desperate to avoid confrontation and conflict. Although women's lives have improved in so many ways over the last 100 years since the days of the suffragette movement, the conditioning passed down through the generations still has a powerful influence on the way we live our lives.

Recent media exposure of high-profile cases of sexual abuse has really brought into sharp focus the true extent to which sexual conditioning has led some men to prey on women. For many women who have experienced unwanted sexual behaviour at the hands of powerful and influential men, the fear of speaking out is very real. After all, there are many potential consequences of doing so and sometimes the personal cost seems too high. In the end it can be easier to do nothing. There is now a new determination on the part of women (and many men) to change these ingrained and insidious attitudes, to strive towards better communication, understanding and respect for each other. But make no mistake

— it will take time because these attitudes run deep, like an underlying disease that not everyone recognises or wants to find a cure for.

This is <u>not</u> a book about either blaming men OR absolving them of their responsibility for the negative impact that inequality still has on society here and across the world. It's about what we as women can do to change the way we respond to it, whether that inequality be real or simply perceived.

Women have grown up under the influence of this culture and we have accepted certain behaviours almost without question — it's just the way it's always been. So we have a responsibility now to know our personal boundaries, what we will and won't put up with, to ensure that we are never inadvertently complicit in this behaviour.

Because we are compliant, helpful and dutiful and we fear getting into trouble, Good Girls can be taken advantage of in many ways.

In the writing of this book I have had conversations with women from many backgrounds. There are cultural differences, of course, but those are somewhat beyond the remit of this book. Let's just say there are Good Girls across the whole of society. In terms of age, for example, both older and younger women seem to be equally affected, despite all the feminist talk over the decades.

So whatever age you are, if this resonates with you, you'll be wanting to get started. Slowly but surely you can begin to change your life for the better. You <u>can</u> free yourself from the crippling grip of 'Good Girl Syndrome' — dump the guilt, begin to live life more fully, and embrace the unique human being that you are. I don't usually quote from ancient religious texts, but I came across this in a recent TED talk by Andrew

Solomon, and it really rings true:

> *'If you bring out what is within you, then what is within you will save you.*
>
> *If you will not bring out what is within you, then what is within you will destroy you.'* GNOSTIC GOSPEL OF ST THOMAS

Before we go any further, I need to address the obvious question — are there no good boys? Yes, there are, because it's all about being expected to be a 'good child'. Boys too can internalise this message at a young age, but because they are also conditioned to be strong and show confidence, as they grow, they are more likely to learn to take risks and push through. Deep down they may remain a Good Boy but by behaving differently they learn not to shrink from life in quite the same way. The key conditioning message for most men is 'be strong', rather than 'be good'. Above all they fear being seen as weak — but that's a different story and a subject for another day!

So, no apologies — this book is about Good Girls. Having said that, though, many of the ideas and techniques here can be used by Good Boys too!

For so many years mine ran the show. Everything I wanted to do or say had to be run past her first. It's all about shame — that's how most Good Girls are created, and mine

> *'She learned to her dismay that she only felt loved when she wasn't being herself.'* JOEL COVITZ, AUTHOR OF 'EMOTIONAL CHILD ABUSE'

was no exception. I'm pretty sure (though the memories are hazy) that the messages in my childhood were very much around 'what will people think', 'play like a Good Girl', 'don't get too big for your boots!' and 'don't show off' (that one I <u>do</u> remember!).

At the root of Good Girl syndrome is the belief that, in order to be loved and accepted we must please others, never mind the cost to ourselves. We are nice, caring and helpful in order to be approved of. We apologise too often — in fact we are so conditioned that we say sorry even when it's clearly the other person's fault! We try to make sure everyone else is okay and ignore how we ourselves are feeling.

We don't want to create waves, make a mistake, upset someone or get into trouble. Taught to be modest, compliant and to keep the peace, we avoid confrontation at almost any cost. We just want to be accepted and loved and it feels as if this is the best way to make that happen. And of course, others are only too happy to take advantage of us! It's important to keep in mind that we teach others how to treat us. When we worry too much about what people might think of us and show too little respect for ourselves, unfortunately they pick up on that and treat us that way too.

The question is, would you rather be seen as 'nice' or respected? It's agonising having to worry all the time about what others are thinking.

I see many clients who have suffered for too long and finally come to the point where something just has to give. Ultimately behaving this way is harmful on so many levels and results in all kinds of emotional and behavioural problems. Depression is common and anxiety can be a constant companion.

On top of all that we can become plagued with anger and resentment. Given that our needs are not being met, it's not so surprising really. And although, ideally, we should think about how we can express it healthily, anger isn't always directed towards the right person. What can happen is that we unconsciously direct it inwards, towards ourselves — after all, we have this deep-down sense of not being good enough, so it feels only fair to blame ourselves when people treat us badly or life throws us curved balls.

Anger is actually a very common emotion in Good Girls, and even though it might not be something we're aware of, it brings many people to therapy because repressed anger tends to lead to depression.

I remember Jayne, always selflessly taking care of her family; looking after her husband's every need, babysitting the grandkids, shopping for her elderly mother, organising family parties — she was a real live wire and the heart of the family. Then ill-health changed all that and suddenly she didn't know who she was any more. Her role had gone because now, however much she might want to, she simply couldn't do it all. She slowly sank into a depression and after seeing a number of mental health professionals, eventually came to see me.

When I asked her if she felt angry, it was like a light bulb moment. Yes! That was exactly how she was feeling! She was angry about everything; with the illness, with her husband for not being supportive enough, and her sons for not understanding her illness. She was especially angry with herself because she could no longer help her family.

But clients don't always feel this sense of relief when we begin talking about anger. They can feel offended at the idea that something as 'ugly' as anger could apply to them. It can take some time to 'confess' to these feelings because until we start exploring what's really going on, we may not have recognised or accepted them.

And once we acknowledge we have these negative feelings towards those around us, into the emotional mix goes — guilt! After all, nice girls don't have these feelings! Well, of course they do, and it's okay to be thoughtless or angry sometimes because you are a fallible human being! The problem comes when we deny how we feel — anger and resentment are powerful emotions that can build to pressure cooker proportions if they are suppressed. They demand to be expressed in some way and often aren't, leaving the Good Girl vulnerable to health issues, both mental and physical. There is sound science to support this.

Just for a moment, bring to mind some people you admire. Do they appear to spend their time being 'nice' and worrying about what others think about them? Or do they bravely go for what they want, not deliberately treading on people's toes but certainly not tiptoeing around them either. They face setbacks and failures, and they just keep going.

EXERCISE: Are your needs being met?

There are many theories about what we need in life to ensure that our emotional needs are being met. One of the diagnostic tools I use with clients is from the Human Givens Institute www.humangivens.com, who say that nature has programmed all of us with physical and emotional needs called 'human givens', without which we cannot be emotionally fulfilled. Our levels of stress depend on how well these needs are being met now and how we deal with the situation when they are not.

The questions they ask are below. Rate, in your judgement, how well the following emotional needs are being met in your life now, on a scale of 1 to 7 (where 1 means not met at all, and 7 means being very well met).

Some of them are quite difficult to answer; just give it your best shot and move on.

1. Do you feel secure in all major areas of your life (such as your home, work, environment)?
2. Do you feel you receive enough attention?
3. Do you think you give other people enough attention?
4. Do you feel in control of your life most of the time?
5. Do you feel part of the wider community?
6. Can you obtain privacy when you need to?
7. Do you have an intimate relationship in your life (one where you are totally physically and emotionally accepted for who you are by at least one person; this could be a close friend)?
8. Do you feel an emotional connection to others?
9. Do you feel you have status that is acknowledged?
10. Are you achieving things and competent in at least one major area of your life?
11. Are you mentally and/or physically stretched in ways which give you a sense of meaning and purpose?

If your scores are mostly low, you are more likely to be suffering stress symptoms, whether emotional, such as depression and anxiety, or as a physical complaint, such as chronic pain. If any need is scored 3 or less, this is likely to be a major stressor for you and even if only one question is marked very low, it can be enough of a problem to seriously affect your mental and emotional wellbeing.

If you're a Good Girl, you can see how easy it might be for many of these needs to go unmet. (One word of caution — make sure that if you've marked No 3 as high that it's balanced with a high score for No 2, and also that you are giving that attention willingly, not because you think you must!!)

So, how long are you prepared to carry on living this way, worrying about others and leaving yourself until last? I finally feel able to do that, but it has taken me decades. My advice is don't wait too long. Make a commitment to yourself to start now, to own all parts of you. Liberated from the insidious influence of your Good Girl you'll try new things, take a few risks and gradually discover that your life is better in so many ways. You will achieve so much more, ideas will flow, and your creativity will come to the fore. You will no doubt start with small steps, but it gets easier and easier.

Changing the way we think and behave, is like changing any other habit; it takes repetition, but stick with the plan and slowly your Good Girl will begin to relax. When she isn't needed any more she can move out of the limelight and finally let you step into it yourself.

Chapter 2
How Did Your Good Girl Develop?

Before we look at the process of changing your default setting, we first need to look at how Good Girls are made. Only then can you get a sense of how yours developed and how, without even realising it, you may have nurtured and reinforced it.

The general consensus seems to be that Good Girls are made, not born, and although our individual personality and temperament may, of course, be a contributing factor, it's likely to be more 'nurture' than 'nature', and it's our childhood experiences that have the most profound influence. In fact, some recent research appears to show that many of the emotional and behavioural characteristics which we have always thought differentiated girls and boys are actually due to conditioning — by parents, in school, by the media, indeed by society in general.

If given the right encouragement, girls can become interested in and develop skills in areas which were traditionally things boys were good at. An example of this is spatial awareness, including making and building. Goodness knows the more girls we can get excited about engineering the better.

Similarly, boys can become more comfortable with their emotions and learn to show more empathy, once they realise they don't have to deny their feelings. There are many differences between men and women, but it seems we aren't hard wired to be as different as we thought. Of course we can't deny the fact that, as a rule, men are physically stronger than women, but I was interested to learn recently that up until the age of seven there is no difference. Girls and boys are equally strong, and yet it seems the children don't realise that.

The conditioning starts so early, is very subtle and it's everywhere.

Your Childhood

As young children we are like blotting paper, absorbing everything around us, and those early impressions from all our senses, sights, sounds, smells, have a profound and lasting impact on us, setting our preferences for life in many ways. Whenever I smell the beautifully fragrant flowers of the Privet bush it takes me back to my four-year-old self, walking down a particular lane to my grandparents' house. I'm sure you have many examples yourself.

We are constantly trying to understand our world and our place in it. For most of us our parents or carers are the main role models in our early life, but older siblings and other family members can also have a profound impact, particularly in larger, close-knit family units. As young children we are at our most impressionable, we readily absorb information about values, beliefs and attitudes, and we develop subconscious prejudices. These messages have a very powerful influence on us and have to a large extent made us who we are today.

In fact, from the moment you were born you began writing the story of your life. Like a stage production with you at the centre, with plot lines, characters, dialogue, different scenes, and plenty of rehearsals! Winner or loser, hero or villain, your script has a powerful impact on your future life — it can empower you, or seriously limit you.

You were taught what to think and feel, and how life should be lived, so that by the age of five or six you had unconsciously created a life plan or script. And that, of course, includes ideas about the way women are treated, the way they themselves should behave and their role both in the family and outside the family. As children we make decisions based on strong emotions, feelings and sensations which have a powerful effect on us. A small baby is acutely aware of expressions, small movements and tone of voice, so if his mother is tense and stiff, he may read this as 'I don't want you too close' or simply 'I don't want you'. Separations can seem life-threatening because you are powerless; after all, your parents create your reality.

> *'It's surprising how many persons go through life without recognising that their feelings towards other people are largely determined by their feelings towards themselves, and if you're not comfortable within yourself, you can't be comfortable with others.'* SYDNEY J. HARRIS

The messages we receive about ourselves, others and the world in general, tend to be simply accepted by us, because at that young age we don't have the intellectual maturity to question the truth of attitudes handed on to us. So if our conditioning tells us that certain behaviours are highly valued, such as being quiet, helpful, kind and well-behaved, we will value them too and we'll comply — after all, all we want is to feel approved of and loved.

I think it's quite likely that your position in the family could also influence the development of your Good Girl. My friend Heidi grew up in Germany as one of eleven children. The first four were boys and she was the eldest of the girls; her role was definitely as a back-up mother. She learnt that she was most appreciated for caring for the other children, so no wonder she grew up to be caring and dutiful. She never ever forgets a birthday and would be mortified if she did.

Eldest daughters often have a more developed sense of responsibility than younger children; expected to be a good example and look after their younger siblings. But whenever we are trying too hard to please others, to gain approval, there's the potential for a Good Girl in the making. Sam told me this: *'I was the youngest of five children, and a twin, something my parents hadn't been expecting. My mother, who had no filter, told me she hadn't wanted another girl. No wonder I was always performing — singing, doing gymnastics in the kitchen to get attention, mainly from my dad who seemed a better bet.'* It won't surprise you to hear Sam grew up to be an actress and singer. She was definitely aiming to be a Good Girl.

Girls seem to focus on these labels more than boys. Historically such qualities have been synonymous with being female. Through the centuries, girls have been taught to defer to and please men, so it's no surprise that these attitudes are still a major influencing factor in most of our lives. Let's face it, parental expectations of boys have always been very different. Unfortunately, attitudes as fundamental and ingrained as these can take a long time to change.

Of course, we are all different and we experience things differently, so even though other children in your family will share many of those beliefs, they will each have created their own individual stories too.

As we reach puberty and our circle widens, we look for people who can take on these roles in our script — and also, we play a role in theirs. We go through life, rewriting this script to fit new situations and environments, but the plot often remains much the same. The good news is that because this is a learnt pattern, it can be changed, and with increasing self-awareness, we can begin to see this illusion for what it is.

Family Dynamics

Let's take a look at some of the many different family dynamics and parenting styles that provide fertile ground for the making of a Good Girl:

<u>Family dominated by Dad.</u> Were you raised in a 'traditional' household where your father made all the decisions, where permission and approval had to be sought from him, and where Mum rarely went against his wishes? Were your brother's ambitions and achievements given greater attention than yours? If so, then you grew up with the ideas that men are more valued than women, that women are inferior.

Perhaps you've never really thought about it before; after all, it was normal for you, and to be fair, it can be quite subtle. Nevertheless, your confidence will have been affected, along with your ability to trust your own instincts and make your own decisions. Often girls in this type of household will go through life feeling somewhat of a victim, instead of someone who takes responsibility for directing her own life.

Alcohol can play a major part in such family dynamics, and in my case my father began drinking when I was about

33

nine years old, when we were stationed in Germany. We trod on eggshells around him and did everything to avoid upsetting him when he had been drinking, because he could be scary, unpredictable and aggressive. We all (including my mum) became very adept at being good, keeping out of the way, and keeping Dad placated. Girls from this kind of family run a real risk later on of being attracted to men with similar problems, because deep down this is how you expect life to be. So having some talking therapy can be worth its weight in gold.

Children brought up in families where there are strict beliefs and rigid rules, will pay a lot of attention to avoiding getting into trouble and being punished. In some religious families the fear of punishment goes as far as the threat of eternal damnation. No wonder these children grow up with anxiety and guilt as constant companions. They will certainly strive to be 'good'.

<u>Anxious, passive or submissive mother</u>. If you grew up with a mother who was anxious and quite passive, a mother who subjugated herself, and for whatever reason put others' needs and desires before her own, this will have been your role model, your template for how women behave. She will have had very little expectation of fulfilling herself or realising her potential.

What does that tell you about *your* value and worth as a female?

Many women come to therapy feeling depressed because after years of trying to please everyone around them, they can't cope any longer. Sometimes they aren't consciously aware of what's wrong with their lives, they just feel defeated. The pleasure they used to get from being needed begins to wear thin as they feel increasingly taken for granted and taken advantage of. The resentment and anger can be almost tangible. If your mother was passive and somewhat submissive, it's quite possible she suffered with depression… and guilt… and a simmering underlying resentment. Let's be honest, that's not conducive to creating a healthy family life.

Unavailable mother. There are many ways in which a mother can be unavailable to her child. She may not be around physically for whatever reason, or she may have been unable to give you the love and emotional nurturing you needed because of her own mental health or psychological problems.

When a parent is depressed, for example, everyone in the family is affected, and to the children of such a family it can be devastating. Depression can suck the life force out of people, leaving them with an agonising emptiness. They often withdraw and cut themselves off from the world around them in an effort at protect themselves from their pain and sadness. But this doesn't solve anything and too often makes things much worse. When we are depressed this is the one thing we mustn't do — we need to interact with those around us in order to get support and help and work our way back to good health.

The depressed mother seems to lose her ability to respond instinctively to her child's needs. She may be able to manage the basic day-to-day care, but joyful interaction, warmth and physical comfort is often missing. A child may wonder what they have done to cause this painful rejection, feeling that in some way it must be their fault, so they try to find ways of making her feel better, protecting her and pleasing her, hoping to make Mum happy again. If this was you, you may have learnt that this was a subject the family avoided talking about, because mental health problems can be associated with shame.

I remember working with Anne, a young woman with

emotional difficulties. We were talking about her background when she became very upset and anxious. She said she had something 'awful' to tell me. It took her a while to pluck up the courage to speak about this terrible secret. 'It's so hard to say this, I haven't ever spoken about it before. When I was ten years old my mother became terribly depressed. Every day when I came home from school, I'd find her still in bed, seemingly unaware of the passing of time or the needs of those around her. I was really frightened and worried about Mum, but I was also ashamed — what if anyone found out? Of course, I couldn't ask any friends back to my house, so eventually I just stopped seeing anyone after school. As time went on I felt more and more isolated and lonely, and it was made worse because my dad didn't talk about it either.' I will never forget how profoundly affected that poor girl still was by what she saw as a terrible, shameful secret.

Alcoholic or drug-addicted parents are also likely to be unavailable, and the child not knowing <u>why</u> is left bewildered, feeling that there is something wrong with them. They think that if they can try harder, perhaps they will be cared for and loved in the way they need to be. These children can develop a kind of guilt that, unchecked, can accompany them through life. In particular they may feel guilty when anyone is feeling unhappy and have a strong urge to 'help' make them better. If alcohol was a problem in your family, there's lots of helpful information from an organisation called 'Adult Children of Alcoholics' https://adultchildren.org/literature/laundry-list/

<u>Rescuer mother.</u> Perhaps your mother was a do-gooder, attracting to her people who needed 'rescuing' in some way. It was her way of feeling valued and needed.

Rose stands out as a really good example of this. Rose

described herself as having been a worrier all her life — she was suffering with anxiety and depression. She had given up her job a few years previously to help Dad care for her mum, who was ill. Sadly, her mother died six months later, and naturally the family was devastated by the loss. Rose then switched her attention to her father. Despite being assured by him that he was doing okay and didn't need her constant attention, she spent virtually every evening at his house, for months on end, leaving her own family on their own at home.

In the meantime, Rose's 17-year-old daughter, who was an only child (and without doubt over-protected and over-indulged), developed an eating disorder. Rose wanted to 'be there for her', which apparently included taking her everywhere in the car, going places with her if she felt anxious (which she often did), preparing her food exactly as stipulated, and so on. You can see the pattern. Then there was the 95-year-old lady who was a friend of a friend and had become dependent on Rose for grocery shopping and for keeping her company!

Despite feeling put upon, exhausted and annoyed, Rose still responded to the elderly lady's apparent emotional blackmail. Needless to say, Rose's husband Mike wasn't getting much attention, and as a result he was distant and spent a lot of time at work! I wasn't surprised that she was suffering with her mental health.

I'm not suggesting for one moment that it's a bad idea to be caring and supportive when others need help, of course not. Where would the human race be if we didn't look out for each other? Kindness really matters, it's vital to our well-being, to feeling connected to others and to binding society together. But it's a matter of degree, and it will be different depending on the circumstances.

To be clear, being supportive is not the same as 'rescuing'. It involves being encouraging rather than 'fixing', being there to listen and help the person work things out for themselves. When you 'rescue', on the other hand, you take over. You set about sorting out their problems for them, as if they will never manage it without you. It's a subtle but important difference. More about that in chapter 9.

Controlling or critical mother. We all strive for control in our lives — it's natural. Without it we feel like leaves blowing in the wind, with no idea of what lies ahead and no way of preparing for it. The important thing is to accept that there are things we can control and things we simply can't, and knowing the difference can be very difficult, for all of us. Having a controlling parent, whether it's your father or mother, is difficult, but a controlling mother can have a more complex and insidious impact, on her daughter in particular.

Many people have told me of the constant criticism from a parent, and this is something you can see played out around you every day. I wonder how many understand the toxic effect of criticism on a child and the profound impact it has on their confidence and future happiness? The drip, drip effect of being told you aren't good enough might lead you to give up completely, or it will create a Good Girl, forever striving for approval.

The root of most controlling behaviour is anxiety, and your mother may have been, for example, so fearful for your safety that you were over-protected. The underlying message to you then is not only that the world is a scary place, but also that you are vulnerable and needy, incapable of sorting your own life out. Even when done with kindness it implies that you are unable to make your own decisions, and that others know better.

One problem is that excessive control is often shown through anger. Naturally all parents get angry — they might be stressed or tired or at their wits' end, but anger is distressing to children and carries a strong 'disapproval' or 'defective' message. This can be very damaging, even more so if violence is part of the parental repertoire.

Families are complicated things and there may have been other, less obvious dynamics at work within your family which led to you becoming a Good Girl. Perhaps your mother always put her own needs first. Perhaps she was envious, resentful or narcissistic, which you will have internalised as being about you, but of course it was really about her, not you. Mothers are indeed powerful, and the effect of a difficult mother can be felt throughout life.

If your mother or father was found wanting, now is the time to understand and forgive them. Remember they were the product of their own upbringing and probably doing the best they could. Being a 'good' parent is quite a challenge for the best of us, and in truth is difficult to define.

I need to emphasise that there are millions of Good Girls out there, and many will not identify with the family issues I describe above. It doesn't matter if you can't identify how yours developed, but if you have the 'symptoms', that's enough to make you officially a Good Girl.

The School Years

It would be easy to blame everything on our parents, but human beings are infinitely complex and there are many factors that play a part in how we develop. As we go through life, all of our experiences influence and change us, so at any point in your development your Good Girl can be switched up a gear. There are many children who have had a happy, stable childhood, but who then suffer terribly at school, often at the hands of their peers. Bullying, which often seems to start during adolescence, can have a devastating and enduring effect on your self-worth. If that happened to you, I feel for you.

It may be that you weren't actively bullied but suffered from more subtle behaviour. I went to 14 different schools in various countries. I was always the new girl, rarely staying long enough to make friends. And it was usually made pretty clear that I wasn't wanted and didn't belong. We've all felt like outsiders at times and we know that can be truly painful. As human beings our ancient instincts for survival are powerful; we are inherently social beings. If early man was rejected by his 'tribe', he was in real danger — danger from predators and also from rival tribes. So it makes perfect sense that we seek the security of belonging.

During your infant and junior school days you probably relished the title of Good Girl; after all, you got lots of approval and positive attention from it! Being occasionally told 'you're so clever', 'you're amazing', or 'so pretty' won't cause too many problems. But, once again it's all about degree — if it seems to be an automatic part of your parents' vocabulary, or you are regularly held up at school as a shining example, it can feel as if you must live up to these accolades at all costs.

If you are a parent, remember it's important to praise effort, not ability — 'that was great work' not 'you're so clever'!

Puberty brings with it an acute awareness of our body,

how we fare in comparison with others, leading us to shine a bright light on our shortcomings. Soon the teenage years come along and with them a different set of challenges, making it difficult to earn the same level of appreciation and praise. This can send self-esteem plummeting and if others see our low self-confidence, they may give us less positive attention, creating a self-fuelling, vicious circle.

In these teenage years Good Girls begin to turn to their friends to have their worth validated and this can take many forms, including trying hard to be popular or funny. Some girls put so much energy into being popular that they can lose their sense of self. It's almost as if they will do anything to achieve it, including gossiping and being unkind, being disloyal and lying. It can also show itself in the form of risky behaviour, for example consenting to sex before they are ready.

> *'Let everything happen to you*
> *Beauty and terror*
> *Just keep going*
> *No feeling is final.'*
> RAINER MARIA RILKE from his poem 'Go to the Limits of your Longing'

Instead of making them feel more confident, it usually does the opposite, reinforcing the idea that they are worthless and making them feel bad about themselves, because when it actually comes down to it we know what feels right and what feels wrong. The choices seem to be, either be true to who you are, and risk being rejected, or strive to conform as the only way to be accepted by others.

There are growing concerns about mental ill-health across the whole of society, and that includes children. I'm so glad that emotional well-being is now being taken more seriously and that counselling is available in more and more schools, across all age groups. In my opinion it should be standard and rolled out everywhere. This is essential if we are to have a mentally healthy population in this frantic world, where the way we live is far removed from the basic design of the human being.

Shame

'(Shame) is an intensely powerful feeling that we are flawed, and therefore unworthy of love or belonging.' BRENÉ BROWN, who writes extensively about shame.

Shame is a basic human emotion familiar to us all. It has its roots in fear and is the foundation upon which your Good Girl was created. We are so afraid of appearing inadequate, of being humiliated, that we don't dare talk about it. Shame is similar to guilt, but where guilt is the feeling that we've done something wrong, shame is the belief that we are intrinsically bad.

It's very common to deal with difficult feelings by suppressing them, but when we do that we also dumb down positive emotions, like joy, hope, inspiration and love, because it's not possible to be selective about which feelings we suppress. And the more we suppress and detach from our feelings, the more they remain locked inside us. What we don't bargain for is that these feelings will not be ignored, and instead of remaining in the past, they insidiously invade our everyday experience of life, becoming more and more troublesome until we acknowledge them and deal with them.

I'm reminded of Philippa who came from a poor family. As a young girl she learnt from her mother that this was something to be ashamed of, so imagine how much greater the shame when her mother sent her off on a bus to ask a relative for money. She was deeply affected by those early years and unsurprisingly the shame she experienced then led to a driving need for financial security. Philippa grew up to be a financial wizard, with a deep-down fear of poverty, which led her to be rigidly controlling around money, causing a lot of friction in her relationships. Funny how she only saw that connection when she began to talk about her childhood, something she had rarely done as an adult. We tend to lock shame away.

Emotions need to see the light of day, to be acknowledged and 'unpacked'. Only then can we begin to feel some relief and reduce their impact. One of my clients put it beautifully when she said they need to be unpacked and then put back more tidily, so we can move on. I love that analogy. If you have a supportive friend that can work well, but if it feels unsafe, please find a good therapist to help you explore difficult feelings.

One thing almost guaranteed to create feelings of intense shame is abuse, be it physical or emotional. These feelings will often lead on to Good Girl behaviour, as you project your lack of self-worth out into the world around you. The shame you experience makes you feel somehow deeply flawed, and you then behave in ways that fit this belief. For some who have been affected in this way, some attention, even negative attention is better than none at all. But abuse is a complex issue, and we don't all respond in the same way; our response will depend on many factors.

The sense of shame that underpins Good Girl Syndrome

often drives a desire for control, for rules, obsessions and perfectionism. This gives a temporary sense of relief from anxiety, but it only masks the real issues. Shame brings with it a fear of showing our true self, preventing us from having meaningful connections with others, and the result is that our own needs remain unmet. We find it so very hard to ask for what we want, to sometimes put ourselves first and to be selfish.

Just think about that for a moment. How would you feel if someone called you selfish? Upset, I'm guessing, because being called selfish is probably one of the most hurtful things you can say to a Good Girl. And anyone who says that to you will be well aware of how much it will hurt. Feeling that life is unfair, that your voice isn't being heard is enough to make anyone upset and angry. You're only human.

We see shame and vulnerability as weakness, but actually our shortcomings are a source of strength once we confront and accept them. When we learn to be more honest and open, it encourages others to be the same, and in that way our communication improves, and we connect at a deeper, more honest level. It has a habit of improving all our relationships, and we feel less isolated. We are more authentic, more human.

Perfectionism

When it comes to perfectionism, studies do show that criticism, whether from parents, teachers or other people in authority, is the main predictor of its development. 'Overly demanding and critical parents put a lot of pressure on kids to achieve,' says Randy Frost, Professor of Psychology at Smith College in Massachusetts, USA. 'Our studies show that is associated with perfectionism.'

And it's not always the most obvious, overt criticism either — as children we are very good at picking up subtle signs of displeasure. That criticism may be accompanied by anger, irritation or disapproval, or it can be as subtle as a roll of the eyes, lift of an eyebrow, or a sigh. I'm sure it will come as no surprise to hear that Good Girls are often perfectionists — it's one of the ways of masking shame and attempting to reduce the anxiety created by Good Girl syndrome.

'Women are often so terrified of being imperfect. They don't want to be laughed at. It holds them back. Young men are taught to take criticism in a kind of impersonal way. Psychologists have documented that women believe approval is like oxygen, which can make it too painful to be a risk-taker or leader because you're too visible and the criticism hurts so much. So one of the things that women need in the next millennium is more inner strength.' NAOMI WOLF, American author and feminist

Perfectionistic personality traits can cause a wide range of difficulties. Typically, those would include difficulty making decisions, dotting i's, crossing t's (checking and rechecking), over-analysing, counting, ruminating, being too picky about potential partners — all common to what psychiatrists refer to as 'obsessive'. Or you can become overly concerned with physical appearance, constantly worrying that you aren't thin enough, tall enough or pretty enough — flawed in some way.

It's actually quite easy to become obsessive about appearance and for it to get out of proportion (forgive the pun). If this is you, you could have what's known as

Body Dysmorphic Disorder (BDD).

You might have BDD if:

- You go to a lot of trouble to conceal imperfections — spending a long time on make-up, hair or choosing clothes.
- You spend a lot of time comparing your looks with other people's.
- You pick at your skin to make it 'smooth'.
- You focus on a certain part of your body, seeing it as flawed, though nobody else agrees with you.
- You weigh yourself often.
- You look at yourself in the mirror frequently or you might avoid mirrors altogether.
- You wear heavy loose clothes to disguise your shape.

We're all a bit obsessive and only a very small proportion of people with this tendency will go on to develop OCD (obsessive compulsive disorder) or BDD, but both are clinical conditions for which you should seek therapeutic help. And similarly, if you are concerned that you might have an eating disorder such anorexia or bulimia, go and seek help from the professionals. You don't need to suffer on your own, and you can be free of this kind of all-consuming anxiety. The sooner you get support the better.

What is perfectionism exactly? The main drive in perfectionism is to avoid failure and, in that way relieve our anxiety. But of course, if you don't fail or make mistakes, then you aren't really living your life — failure helps us grow. I believe it is in overcoming failure and disappointment that we learn most about ourselves and how to live our best life. If you are a perfectionist, it might surprise you to hear that your main drive is <u>not</u> about succeeding, it's actually about not failing. There's a big difference. A healthy 'high achiever' on the other hand accepts they won't always get things right. So they avoid the chronic anxiety and stress that accompanies perfectionism and instead are free to enjoy their successes!

Because few things are ever perfect, it's an impossible goal which in your mind you will always fall short of. Perfectionists are not happy people. They can't allow themselves to bask in the pleasure of their achievements or really enjoy their relationships, driven as they are, by the pressure they put on themselves. Nothing is ever quite good enough. They also tend to be cautious and risk averse, which means they won't try new things or take on a new challenge unless they know they will succeed. You know, those people who say, 'I never try anything unless I know I'll be good at it.'

There is one aspect of perfectionism called Socially Prescribed Perfectionism which is very familiar to the Good Girl. As well as putting a lot of internal pressure on themselves Good Girls worry excessively about what other people think. They assume that others are judging them as harshly as they judge themselves! The thought of asking a neighbour to turn their TV down, or of saying the wrong thing in a meeting at work would fill them with horror!

It's easy to see how this can lead to crippling social anxiety — they are increasingly nervous in unfamiliar settings and gradually find themselves avoiding social situations of any kind. But the trouble is that, although avoiding difficult situations feels like a relief at the time, actually it just re-enforces your belief that you 'can't' and you feel even more anxious and stressed the next time you face something similar.

I often remind myself that '**good enough is indeed good enough**'.

> '*Perfectionism is the voice of the oppressor, the enemy of the people. It will keep you cramped and insane your whole life and is the main obstacle between you and that shitty first draft. I think perfectionism is based on the obsessive belief that if you run carefully enough, hitting each stepping stone just right, you won't have to die. The truth is that you will die anyway and that a lot of people who aren't even looking at their feet, are going to do a whole lot better than you, and have more fun while they're doing it.*' ANNE LAMOTT, author of 'Bird by Bird, Some Instructions on Writing and Life'

Chapter 3
The Life of a Good Girl

Your inner Good Girl began terrorising you very early in life and because of that you will experience her mainly at a subconscious level. In fact, like a thread running all the way through the very fabric of who you are, she feels like an intrinsic part of you, part of your identity. So much so that you might wonder: who would I be without her? The truth is, once you've identified the offending thread, given a little patience and time, it can be gently and carefully removed, allowing you to be a better, happier, more complete version of yourself!

Because our Good Girl is subconsciously influencing and driving so much of how we feel, how we think, and how we behave, it stands to reason that she has the potential to affect all areas of our life. But, because we are all different, some of us will be more vulnerable to her influence in say, our love relationships than at work, or with our friends.

If you stop and think about it for a moment, you'll know when you're in her grip. For example, when you waste a lot of time and energy over-thinking, agonising about what to do or what to say, because you're afraid of getting it wrong or upsetting someone. Most of all, and at all costs, you want to avoid confrontation or conflict. Using so much time and energy avoiding difficult situations or possible pitfalls means that Good Girls miss out on so much.

When you are constantly holding back, afraid to show your true self, how can you relax around others? Remember what Good Girls fear most of all is shame and rejection and we're afraid that if we are seen as unkind, selfish or thoughtless we'll be exposed as 'not very nice' — and how dreadful that would be!

Ellie was telling me that she had been feeling low, but found it difficult to talk to friends about it because she didn't want to burden them, and also because actually <u>she</u> was the one everyone came to with <u>their</u> problems! So she was doing a great job listening and supporting others, but not allowing them to do the same for her. She wasn't really being very honest. Good Girls like Ellie go to great lengths to avoid exposing their vulnerabilities, afraid of what it might reveal about them. But paradoxically it's doing this very thing that allows us to be real with others.

Imagine how great it will be to feel less like a victim, to be able to ignore the inner critic that puts so much pressure on you to be a certain way. Just to be clear, not all Good Girls are timid and beaten down by fears. Far from it. For many the drive to prove themselves provides a disguise and most people will be unaware that underneath that apparent confidence is a crippling fear of failure, because the signs are easy to miss. Think about someone you know who seems pretty confident, but they try too hard and tend to take things too seriously. They are defensive when under pressure and often seem stressed. That's a Good Girl right there — but incognito.

Wouldn't it be wonderful to stop caring so much about what other people might think? To be more open and trusting. How liberating to feel less responsible, to leave guilt behind, to say no when you want to, to put your own needs first and finally feel 'good enough'. I want to get you so excited by the promise of change that you will begin this new journey determined to live that change.

EXERCISE: Just How Much of a Good Girl are You?

The following questions will help you identify to what extent that Good Girl is running your life. Be brutally honest with yourself.

Read each statement and then decide which number on the scale of 1 — 5 most reflects your assessment of yourself.

1 = never true   *2= rarely true*   *3= sometimes true*

4= often true   *5= always true*

1.	I rarely behave selfishly or in a demanding way	
2.	I find it difficult to express anger	
3.	I often give a compliment when I don't really mean it	
4.	I am careful how I say things so people will like me	
5.	Asking for what I want is hard for me	
6.	I find myself obsessing about the finer details of a task	
7.	I often doubt myself	
8.	I often feel emotionally vulnerable	
9.	When someone gives me negative feedback I feel criticised and upset	
10.	I avoid possible conflict or confrontation	
11.	I can't bear it if I might have upset or hurt someone	
12.	I have friends/acquaintances whom I only see because I feel I should	
13.	I avoid saying what I really think	
14.	I put off facing situations which might be awkward	

15.	I often feel people take advantage of me	
16.	I take care of other people's needs before my own	
17.	If I make a mistake, I feel really bad	
18.	I apologise too often	
19.	I agonise over making decisions	
20.	I often feel ashamed, embarrassed or self-conscious	
21.	I worry excessively about what people think of me	
22.	I feel guilty when I take time for myself	
23.	I often get talked into doing things because I can't say no	
24.	I want to be thought of as a nice person	
25.	I avoid social situations because I feel intensely uncomfortable	
26.	I feel inferior to people who appear more attractive or successful than me	
27.	Worrying thoughts often go round and round in my head	
28.	If I have to speak in public, I feel extremely anxious	
29.	I try too hard to prove my competence	
30.	I probably take myself too seriously	
	TOTAL	

Now add your scores together:

30 — 53 Little or no Good Girl

53 — 76 Mild to moderate Good Girl

76 — 100 Moderate to strong Good Girl

100 — 124 Strong to very strong Good Girl

124 — 150 Very strong Good Girl

I'm guessing that your result doesn't really surprise you. I know questionnaires can be difficult because some of the statements might be more true of you at work than with your family, for example. However, this gives us a good enough overview of how much your Good Girl is affecting your life and your ability to live it free of emotional obstacles. Let's take a look at the different areas of your life and identify, which aspects of it are being affected the most.

Love Life

Bernadette was a woman who you would never have had down as a Good Girl. At work she could be brutal in her determination to get her own way and was known throughout the company as someone who was only too happy to lock horns if you questioned her. To be honest, she was quite a bully, but it was hard to challenge her because (damn it) she was exceptionally good at her job. What's more, when she wanted to be charming, she could most certainly turn it on.

One summer we were invited to a charity BBQ being organised by her and her husband David at their village hall. The event was going well. They were great hosts, and David came across as charming. There was, however, a moment during the evening which afforded me an unexpected insight into her home life. I can see it now — as she placed a plate of food in front of David, his face darkened. 'That burger looks cold.' he said, 'I suppose you just grabbed it off the table! You idiot, you should have waited for one fresh from the BBQ. You know I hate cold food! And I can't stand that wholegrain mustard either, you know that....' Bernadette flinched, but quickly recovered her composure. Smiling and apologising, she went to get him another burger.

Around David she became the subservient little wife who was desperate to please him — basically if David said 'jump', she said 'How high?' So, she had a Good Girl in there, and that was quite a revelation. Now I began to see her differently — I saw her vulnerability and felt a little compassion for her. At work she was afraid of not being seen as the best, and at *home she was constantly looking for approval. So again, it was all about not feeling good enough and her drive to prove that she was. Of course, she <u>was</u> already good enough, she just didn't feel it.*

Because Bernadette was vulnerable and needy when it came to love, she had unconsciously been attracted to a controlling man. The way he treated her reinforced her deep-down conviction that she was flawed, didn't really deserve better and had to try hard to please him. Men like this, often narcissistic, enjoy belittling women because it makes them feel more powerful and they can temporarily forget their own inadequacies and fears. Instead of pursuing weak women as one might expect, they often choose women who are perceived as strong because the challenge is greater and victory that much sweeter.

The problem is that controlling behaviour can be quite subtle, and particularly in the beginning you might find yourself questioning if it's worth making a fuss over his demands, because after all perhaps it doesn't really matter that much. Then before you know it, it's happening more and more often.

The typical narcissist will show up disguised as a hero, or a prince coming to the rescue, bearing flowers and romantic promises, charming the birds from the trees. So it's easy to see how we can easily become entranced by all that flattery and attention — after all, being put on a pedestal makes you feel great about yourself! The trouble with pedestals is that they are so easy to fall off — and that's when things can begin to go wrong. It seems that whatever you do is wrong and the need for control becomes more oppressive. You end up spending so much time and energy focusing on pleasing him that you may not even know what your own needs are any more. In a way you lose touch with yourself and who you are.

You can find yourself cooking what he likes, seeing less of your own friends, wearing what he likes, going on holidays that he likes, buying furniture that he likes and finding that your own career now takes a back seat. Because you hate conflict you don't ask for what you want or say what you think. Or if you do, it's in a passive aggressive way — you say it indirectly, perhaps under your breath; you sulk, nag, but you don't deal with it honestly and assertively. (There's plenty about how to change that later in the book.) This situation is feeding your fears about not being good enough and slowly eroding your self-confidence.

> *'Remember always that you not only have the right to be an individual, you have an obligation to be one.'* ELEANOR ROOSEVELT

Many women stay in these relationships because they have been manipulated and subliminally persuaded to believe the criticisms levelled at them by their partner, which makes it hard to find the courage to leave and move on. Remember this — looking to others to make you feel better about yourself simply won't work.

Being in a relationship like this can also make it very hard to ask for support from friends and family because you may feel embarrassed or ashamed. You may come across as strong and capable, but you feel foolish — and let's face it, it's not easy to admit to having made a mistake. So we avoid the subject and do our best to cover it up. Of course, given time people do tend to notice these things but they don't want to be intrusive — after all, none of us really knows what goes on privately between couples and it feels like a no-go area to 'pry'.

Having said all this, there is no doubt that relationships are complicated. Successful partnerships depend on many things, but the willingness to compromise, to give and take are essential ingredients. You can't have our own way all the time, but nor should your partner. So you must be prepared to stand up for yourself and not to shy away from confrontation. One of the qualities of a healthy relationship is that you can handle disagreement and conflict. Of course, if there is a threat of conflict becoming physical or if you feel bullied or threatened at any time, that's not healthy and you're best to remove yourself from the situation, temporarily at least.

The Thorny Issue of Sex

Earlier I talked about the Good Girl's attitude towards being 'perfect', including having the perfect body. Whereas on a rational level we probably understand that we all have 'imperfectly perfect' bodies, at an emotional level, if we're honest, most of us feel that we are flawed. Unsurprisingly feeling ashamed and embarrassed by your body will badly affect your ability to relax, to forget yourself, let go, be playful and enjoy sexual intimacy.

The truth is that probably most of us find it difficult to talk to our partner about sex — I suspect it's one of the world's most avoided conversations! But if we don't, then how can we develop true intimacy? How can we let each other know what we like or dislike, or say when we do or don't feel like having sex? The problem is often that we're not even honest with ourselves, which makes it pretty difficult to be honest with anyone else.

Sexual intimacy is an important part of a long-term relationship, and shame, especially body shame, can create real obstacles to sexual pleasure. This will be particularly so if you were brought up to think of sex as 'dirty' and to regard those parts of your body as secret, something intensely private or to be ashamed of. It goes without saying that if you were sexually abused as a child, this will almost certainly have left you with complicated feelings and attitudes towards sexual contact.

Later we'll see how learning to have compassion for yourself, learning to love and accept yourself will allow you to truly express yourself more fully, in every way.

Dealing with your ex

If you (or those close to you) have separated or divorced after a long relationship, and especially if you have children, you'll be very familiar with the emotional and practical stresses involved. Initially there are the issues of sorting out accommodation, splitting possessions and finances, but that is far from the end of it. If you have children, too often there's the ongoing strain of organising access, even where both partners are being reasonable.

But if your ex is demanding or manipulative, it's really important to stand your ground. We've all heard stories of ex-partners changing arrangements to suit them, being unreliable or not sticking to parenting agreements. I know it sounds a bit harsh, but if you don't clarify boundaries and speak up assertively, then, in a way, you only have yourself to blame when they take liberties. Remember this could go on for many years. Respecting your own rights and putting the child's needs first are key principles and you need to be able to communicate that loud and clear. Later on I'll show you how.

Family Life

Good Girls are dutiful. When elderly parents need caring for you can be fairly sure that it's the Good Girl who steps up and, before she knows it, finds herself responsible for much more than she expected. And I'm afraid that other siblings will often be only too happy to let them get on with it. Please don't misunderstand me — many people really enjoy looking after their elderly parents (my daughter says she will, which I am naturally grateful for!). They feel enriched by the experience and are glad they can give back to those who gave so much to them.

But we are all different and for some, for many different reasons, it is a huge strain. We may be doing the caring out of an over-developed sense of responsibility or guilt. Or the 'rescuer' role is one we fall into very easily as a way of feeling temporarily better about ourselves, ignoring our real issues. It's easy then to feel like a martyr, to feel unappreciated and vacillate between 'rescuer' and 'victim'.

Parenting

From the moment you are handed that little bundle of joy your life changes for ever. For some women the anxiety they experience at that time can become a habit that they unwittingly allow to get out of hand. Anxiety spreads seamlessly from one area of your life to another if left unchecked and there seems to be so much to worry about these days! Remember Good Girls fear getting it wrong. There is no manual telling you the definitive way to be a mother and absolutely everyone has an opinion about how to care for your child.

Because we care so much and we don't want to cause upset, we can fall into the habit of giving in too often. We forget the importance of boundaries, of saying 'no', of teaching children to manage their impulses and so on. We love them so much we don't want to deny them anything and we kill them with kindness. Being 'cruel to be kind' has a somewhat harsh ring to it, but the point is that despite how it feels, we need to find a way to stand firm. Children need boundaries now and in the future. And despite their protestations this helps them to feel secure.

The desire to protect our children from being upset can easily go too far. By being overly protective we teach them to be fearful, to lack confidence, to avoid taking risks and struggle with decisions.

To thrive in this increasingly frantic world of ours, one of the most vital qualities they need is resilience — to bounce back from disappointments, mistakes and failure. To know they are already good enough. That they can trust themselves to make good decisions, that it's okay to make mistakes because that's how we learn.

We must ourselves be good role models for our children, otherwise we risk creating yet another generation of Good Girls. Show them it's important to take time for themselves, to relax and practise self-care. Tell them they don't have to worry too much about what others think of them, that the house doesn't always have to be tidy, that we don't need to have everything our friends have. Teach them to have the courage to speak up. 'Good enough' parenting means our kids will probably turn out pretty well. Try to be that 'good enough' role model.

Social Life

Your Good Girl has a field day in social situations. It might surprise you to hear that social anxiety (or shyness, same thing really) is the most common of the anxiety disorders, so if this is you, you're definitely not alone. We all have insecurities — ultimately human beings are not that much different from each other and we all struggle at times. Believe me, just because you can't see others' internal struggles doesn't mean they don't have them.

The problem is that, instead of being open, relaxed and genuinely interested in other people, you can become absorbed in your own version of reality. That 'inner critic' can be crippling, convincing you of your flaws, worries and insecurities. You will be anxious about saying the wrong thing, looking stupid or embarrassing yourself, so that you avoid engaging in conversation, and instead remain in the background as a way of staying 'safe'.

But as I mentioned earlier this avoidance actually maintains and fuels the fear. Avoiding situations, avoiding giving an opinion, avoiding eye contact — all this keeps us feeling anxious. It's important to remember this — we gain confidence through action, not through avoidance. Through facing our fears and acting as if we're confident we gain evidence that we can do it.

Take a moment now to think about the image you have of yourself in social situations. I imagine it's a negative one. The way you see yourself is vital to your confidence, and I really hope that you will do the exercises in this book to help you change that image to a more realistic and positive one.

In your closer friendships, are you sometimes too empathic and keen to be liked that you inadvertently give them permission to offload onto you? It might feel good that others tell you their troubles, as long as you tell them yours too.

Social Media

This is a whole subject in itself. We all know social media is artificial, that it's by no means a true reflection of reality, yet we somehow get sucked in anyway. The problem is if you aren't in a good place in your own life, it's a painful reminder of how 'apparently' happy everyone else is. They have more friends (no-one has that many 'friends'), a better social life, a perfect partner, more expensive 'stuff'… more 'likes'. Don't you believe it. We all edit what we put on social media, only including the bits we want people to see.

> *'Social media has become a space in which we form and build relationships, shape self-identity, express ourselves, and learn about the world around us; it is intrinsically linked to mental health.'*
> SHIRLEY CRAMER CBE, Chief Executive, RSPH

If you're a young woman, you won't remember a life without social media, but it will have had a huge influence on you. In 2017 a survey conducted by the Royal Society for Public Health asked 14-24 year olds in the UK how social media platforms impacted their health and wellbeing. The survey results found that Snapchat, Facebook, Twitter and Instagram all led to increased feelings of depression, anxiety, poor body image and loneliness. YouTube topped the table as the most positive.

It's a great way to keep in touch with friends and family, to reach out when you feel isolated, but it is also a very effective tool for manipulation and torture. I know it's tempting to go looking for photos of his new girlfriend or check to see what your friends have been doing without you... but let's be honest, it will probably hurt.

Or you could make a decision to stop now — that's the grown-up thing to do.

Working Life

This is a part of your life where you really do need to be in 'adult' mode pretty much all the time. That involves being straight, assertive, standing your ground and speaking up for yourself. It means not taking criticism to heart, not assuming you know what people are thinking of you, and not taking things personally. Your Good Girl needs to stay quiet and instead of reacting emotionally, you connect with your thinking self. This then allows you to disagree or perhaps admit you don't understand something.

If you constantly worry about doing or saying the right thing, you're likely to spend too much time lost in the detail, fixated on making it perfect and ignoring the bigger picture. You'll find decisions painful and procrastinate much too often.

Early in my working life I remember being in a big meeting, where I felt out of my depth. To my horror (I can still feel it now as I write), during that meeting my boss turned to me and asked me to take on one of the tasks being discussed. There was only one problem — I had no idea what he meant! Now, if I had simply swallowed my pride and gone to see him afterwards to ask for help, I could have avoided all the stress and wasted time that followed. In fact, I would probably have earnt his trust and gone up in his estimation.

Good Girls are usually so busy seeking approval — they stay late, volunteer to help too often and are easy to take advantage of. They play safe, avoid risk and feel anxious when change is afoot — but, of course, change is an intrinsic part of modern working life. You would so love to relax and be yourself but you're afraid to show any individuality or creativity. What a shame!

Then there's the ultimate challenge — speaking in public or giving a presentation! Horror of horrors — the mere thought of it will send most Good Girls into a panic, desperate to find a way out of it. The problem is that as your career progresses this is likely to be unavoidable.

It's such hard work covering up your insecurities, leaving you with too little energy to pursue your goals. So, who would want to be that 'nice girl' who apologises too often and tries too hard to be liked?

Chapter 4
Stress, Anxiety and the Good Girl

'*You can't stop the waves, but you can learn how to surf.*' Jon Kabat-Zinn

Stress is on the rise and so is mental ill health. All the research tells us that. We may have less hardship and disease than our ancestors, but the pressure on us seems greater than ever. The pace of life today is phenomenal. We all have to work harder, faster, longer and more efficiently, and job security is a thing of the past.

Technology and the internet mean that we have access to an infinite amount of information, which is totally brilliant if like me you grew up with a set of encyclopaedias! But this can feel overwhelming for Good Girls as it intensifies the feeling that they can never ever know enough. We can be reached at any time and are in contact with a many more people than in the traditional working day of the past, and that means there are potentially so many more people to please. The Good Girl's unrealistic expectations of herself are sent into overdrive!

Our expectations have increased along with the range of choices available to us. So much has changed over the last 50 years. There was a time when we each knew our 'place' in life, defined mainly by gender, where we lived and what kind of work our fathers did. Doctor or miner, you were likely to follow a similar path, and probably not move too far from your home town. As a woman you were almost certainly going to be a housewife.

Families today are often spread far and wide, which means we have less access to the wisdom passed down through the generations.

Many people hardly know their neighbours, so communities don't exist in the way they once did, and many more of us live alone. In the past religion provided comfort and a sense of community. It reinforced your place in society — not always comfortable but it did provide a sense of security, nevertheless. Support is an important factor in staying mentally healthy — we can cope with a lot more when we feel the support of those around us.

> *'Where is the wisdom we have lost in knowledge? Where is the knowledge we have lost in information?'* T.S. ELIOT

As our 'fight or flight' response, stress is very effective if we need to fight the advancing army or make a hasty retreat, but not so appropriate when faced with a difficult boss or the prospect of having to give a presentation at work!

There are lots of different definitions of the word 'stress', but in a nutshell it's pressure we feel we can't cope with. As the 1st century philosopher Epictetus said, 'People are disturbed not by things, but the views they take of them.' So it's our perception of what's going on for us, and whether or not we feel we can cope with it, that leads us to feel stressed or anxious, as opposed to what is actually going on in our lives. We each live in our own reality 'tunnel', and everything we think and feel is seen from our own unique perspective. It's all about the meaning you make of things.

How we interpret life's problems and pressures depends very much on our individual beliefs and attitudes. Make no mistake, what you think of as reality is merely your own interpretation of it and it is almost certainly different from everyone else's! More on that later.

Go back to eating the grass

Whether antelope or human being, when we sense danger, our fear instinct kicks in and within a split second we switch into the 'fight or flight' response. There are effectively two pathways in the brain that can cause anxiety. One begins in the cerebral cortex, the large 'thinking' part of the brain that involves perceptions and thoughts. The other travels directly to a part of the brain called the amygdala, a small structure deep in the brain that triggers the fight or flight response.

Early humans had a very strong fear response; after all, being cautious meant you were more likely to survive and pass your genes on to future generations. Perhaps we should take a moment to be grateful to our watchful, super-alert ancestors!

In the same way that the antelope will experience a surge of neurochemicals and hormones at the moment he realises he is in danger (principally adrenaline, noradrenaline and cortisol), so do we. Our body switches into survival mode and the basic fear instinct takes over. Our blood supply is redirected to the heart and major muscles; heart rate and respiration increase; blood pressure increases; fats and sugars are released; digestion slows right down; pupils dilate;

sweating increases... and so on.

Once the danger is over the antelope goes back to eating the grass and all is well. And that's very much the same for us if we have to run to avoid being run over by a lorry — we react in a split second and then relax once we're safe. However, if you've had an argument with your partner or lost your car keys, you're unlikely to actually *use* that surge of physical energy, and you're left to 'stew' in those stress chemicals. The body does, however, gradually return to normal, of course.

The problem comes when this is happening so often that we become over-sensitised to it. This heightened state of awareness or hyper-stimulation creates a kind of chronic stress, where our bodies take much longer to return to normal and it is that which can lead to all kinds of physical and mental problems. In order to slow us down our body gives us the 'gift' of illness — it is estimated that at least 75% of visits to the family doctor are in some way stress-related. Stress affects our work, our relationships and our ability to enjoy life.

We are only just beginning to recognise (or rediscover) the vastly complex relationship between our biology, genes and emotions, but there is no doubt that our Good Girl plays a significant part in the development and maintenance of stress, so I make no apologies for devoting time to the subject.

Stress affects each of us differently, depending on our personality, background and experiences in life, and because we are all unique individuals the symptoms will vary — some will have more physical signs (e.g. headaches, back pain), others more emotional signs (e.g. easily upset, anxious) and others may have a predominance of behavioural symptoms (e.g. shouting, drinking too much). Take a moment now to consider how stress might be affecting you.

The female brain and anxiety

Anxiety is one of the symptoms of stress, and we all know how it feels, because it's a normal, natural human emotion; it's nature's way of keeping us safe. It is, however, becoming the most common mental health condition globally. A rapidly growing problem, it affects people from all backgrounds and all walks of life, and across cultures. Its fundamental purpose is to protect us; by causing us to reflect on past experiences before we act and to prepare us for potential problems. However, it's a bit like a silent epidemic — its symptoms often develop over many years, ranging from passing feelings of nervousness to full-blown panic attacks, and left unchecked it can become an ingrained habit, which is hard to break.

We worry... about what people think of us, about what might happen and might not happen. Then we worry about worrying... and if we're not careful, we can gradually find ourselves avoiding more and more situations. This negative downward spiral drains our energy, leading to depression, and that in turn makes the anxiety worse.

So why is it that some of us are prone to feeling anxious and others aren't? There is almost certainly some genetic predisposing component to anxiety, making some of us more alert or hyper-vigilant. These are the people who metaphorically stand on the ramparts of the castle scanning with a searchlight for the advancing army.

What about gender? As you've probably guessed women are more vulnerable to both depression and anxiety; in fact, research shows that for roughly every three cases of anxiety, two of them will be women. The statistics for depression are much the same, and as I mentioned, the two conditions often go hand in hand, one reinforcing the other. If you think about our early ancestors, it was generally the females who were responsible for caring for children and the elderly, and for maintaining harmony within the group. We have developed to be more sensitive to our environment, to be alert to potential danger to our children, to have greater emotional awareness and also to respond more emotionally.

The way we respond to stress is different too. In women it tends to be the left side of the brain (the 'flight' side) that responds more readily to stress. This side is more responsible for careful thought, evaluating detail, weighing up pros and cons etc, so it's no wonder we worry. Sarah McKay, author of *The Women's Brain Book* explains that we are more prone to 'internalising disorders', such as panic disorders, social anxiety, phobias, post-traumatic stress disorder (PTSD), OCD, eating disorders and so on. That internal negative self-talk tends to be more unkind and more self-critical in females than males. As women, when depressed we are more likely to lose our appetite, have low energy and feel more pain.

Men, however, are more inclined to react to stress with the right side of the brain (the 'fight' side). They are more likely to have 'externalising disorders' such as problems with alcohol, drugs, aggression or violence — all action-related behaviours as opposed to internal ruminations and over-thinking, more common in women.

Please do remember, although this book is about Good Girls, that these are generalisations between men and women and there is plenty of overlap between the sexes.

Good Girls worry — a lot!

'Worry never robs tomorrow of its sorrow, it only saps today of its joy.' LEO F. BUSCAGLIA

When we worry it's usually about the future, thinking about what *might* happen, and often involves a 'what if...' style of thinking. This includes lots of speculation, jumping to conclusions and fortune-telling. Considering one of the Good Girl's greatest fears is not meeting her own high standards, and being disapproved of, worrying is likely to be a constant companion. As women it seems we are more likely to ruminate, allowing thoughts to go round and round in our heads, sometimes feeling they will drive us mad. And too much rumination is well known as a cause of both depression and anxiety. It tends to foster feelings of hopelessness, pessimism, shame and guilt. It is more associated with constantly running over a *past* event — for example, that important meeting where you said something you wish you hadn't. Good Girls are really adept at torturing themselves about what they 'should' have done or said! It's a kind of retrospective need for control, as if we can change it by replaying it over and over again!

I remember when I first began my monthly appearances on BBC radio, as their resident Agony Aunt. After each show I found myself 'agonising' over what I'd said or what I'd left out. I went over and over everything. I played my mental video clip of the situation and often succeeded in making myself feel quite miserable, despite the positive things people said about how it went. The revelation came when it dawned on me that most people had more important things to do than to hang onto *my* every word, and the fact that they kept asking me back year after year meant I must surely have been good enough! And good enough is indeed good enough! Say it after me — you need to remember it.

GOOD ENOUGH IS GOOD ENOUGH

If we can't put past events behind us (having first learnt what we need to learn from them, of course), then they will affect us in the future, causing pointless emotional pain and lack of engagement in our daily lives. It will also make us reluctant to try new things and take risks.

We all know that these anxious thoughts can be so difficult to turn off. They are often just below the level of conscious thought, almost like a constant background noise that we only become aware of intermittently. They can leave us with a sense of foreboding, dragging us down and depleting our energy. These intrusive thoughts along with unhelpful images can run like a looping piece of film, creating a kind of vicious circle, making us feel more anxious and fearful. In fact, when we 'fret' the brain interprets that as stress and sends out more stress hormones to cope with the 'crisis'. All of this over-thinking is such hard work!

> '*The mind is its own place, and in itself can make a heaven out of hell, and a hell out of heaven.*' MILTON, Paradise Lost

It's amazing how easily we can upset ourselves through the thoughts and images in our heads. In fact, the primitive part of our mind can't distinguish between what is real and what is imagined, so our body responds accordingly, releasing stress hormones just as if it is *really* happening now. And the more vividly we imagine these things, the more tense we become and the worse we feel. The more aware you are of how your thoughts are feeding your worrying habit, the better — it's important to develop the ability to stand back and observe your 'thinking' self. We'll be working on this later, but let's make a start now. Whenever you notice yourself worrying, try 'tuning' into your thoughts. Are you thinking negatively? What images are you playing?

The Effects of Worrying

The way in which worry affects us varies with the individual, but let's look at some of the most common effects. Something that we all have problems with now and again is sleep, and it comes as no surprise then that chronic worries can lead to problems getting to sleep, as well as disturbed sleep, waking early in the morning and not being able to get back to sleep. People often complain of chronic muscle tension making it really difficult to relax; generalised anxiety; feelings of nervousness; restlessness; headaches; lack of concentration —the symptoms go on and on.

The key to dealing with anxiety is to catch it early so it doesn't spiral out of control. At regular intervals throughout the day, take a moment to scan your body for signs of tension. That way you can take some action to prevent it from building up — you can take back control before it escalates.

Many of us carry around this excess of nervous energy. Some may come across as high achievers, perfectionists, in control and calm. But this tension has to go somewhere, so it leaks out in the form of foot tapping, nail biting, finger picking, nervous laughter, tight shoulders or ongoing mild stomach problems. Believe me, the workplace is full of people desperately trying to hide their insecurities!

It's important to look for ways to channel that energy. Most of all, acknowledge your vulnerability and accept yourself as a normal fallible human being.

A word about panic attacks

Sudden feelings of panic are very unpleasant — if you've ever had what is generally called a panic 'attack', you will know that. The first thing to note is that this is not an 'attack' in any way.

However bad it might feel, panic is **not dangerous**. You might feel you're going to choke, have a heart attack or faint, but it is simply an over-enthusiastic stress response. The adrenaline and other stress hormones are released as if your life were being threatened.... but it isn't. You notice the physical sensations, like the feeling of tightness in your throat or a pounding heart, and that leads to a vicious cycle of panicky thoughts and more physical sensations. The feeling will pass (as it always does), and once you give it less importance, it immediately seems less threatening.

How to Handle a Panic Attack:
- No need to be afraid. Flow through it. It will pass as it has before. This will significantly reduce its power.
- Move your body. This changes your physiological state.
- Tell yourself something positive.
- Actively do something else; it doesn't matter what! Turn your attention elsewhere.

There are some really effective instant techniques for interrupting feelings of panic if you read a little further on.

Changing your brain chemistry

You might wonder how knowing about the chemistry of

anxiety can possibly help with your problems. Bear with me, because understanding the basic science can really help you get to grips with anxiety and depression.

The neurobiology of anxiety is highly complex, but our understanding of how the brain works is increasing at a rapid rate. What's more, with the arrival of the MRI machine we can now actually watch the brain at work.

Simply put, neurotransmitters are the 'messenger' chemicals in your brain — they allow electrical impulses to pass between neurons (or nerves). Some are 'exciters' and some are 'inhibitors', and it's all about getting the balance right. Here are some of the key players:

GABA (Gamma-aminobutyric acid) has a calming effect on the brain. It improves mental focus and helps the brain to filter out background noise. Meditation, deep relaxation and yoga have been shown to increase the natural production of GABA. To increase levels through your diet, it is important to eat glutamate-rich food such as bananas, halibut, almonds, oranges, lentils, oats, rice bran, potatoes, walnuts and spinach, to name but a few.

Seratonin, often called 'the happiness hormone' helps to regulate your mood and keep stress under control. It also has a positive effect on libido, sleep, memory and learning as well as a variety of other functions. Exercise and exposure to light activity are the main ways to increase production (massage is also helpful), but what also works is remembering positive, happy events that have happened in your life. This simple act increases serotonin production in the anterior cingulate cortex, which is a region just behind the prefrontal cortex that controls attention. The same study also found that remembering sad events decreased serotonin production.

Dopamine is part of the brain's 'reward system' and creates feelings of satisfaction or pleasure when we do things we enjoy, such as eating, having sex, listening to music or completing a great piece of work. Drugs like cocaine, nicotine, heroin, and alcohol increase levels of dopamine but, of course, will bring with them much greater problems!

Endorphins are produced by the brain in response to pain. They are our body's natural painkillers but can also help in the quest to reduce anxiety. Everyone's heard of 'runner's high', the wonderful feeling of ecstasy when you run really hard. Vigorous exercise, laughter…and chocolate are a few ways of elevating your endorphins!

Oxytocin is often called the 'love hormone'. Produced when we hug, kiss or make love, its creation is also very important during childbirth, promoting bonding with the baby and milk production. When we fall in love, that first flush of heady romance is accompanied by plenty of oxytocin, so much so that it can be quite addictive. It calms us and has been shown to make the amygdala (responsible for emotional processing and associated with fear) less reactive.

Having a pet to love and care for also results in higher oxytocin levels. In fact, research has shown that when you stroke your dog, not only do you release oxytocin, so does your dog! Everybody wins. So hug someone or get a pet! Alternatively, we can create feelings of love by simply focusing on loving thoughts. After all, our brain doesn't know the difference between 'imagined' feelings and 'real' feelings! So, the great news is that there are many ways in which you can influence this hormone balance in order to reduce anxiety, improve your mood and increase feelings of well-being.

Rewiring your brain

As a Good Girl you will be no stranger to a range of emotions — anxiety, shame, guilt, hurt, frustration, anger, embarrassment and many more. And although it feels like it, you aren't at the mercy of them — they don't happen to you, your brain creates them. Emotions aren't built into our brains at birth; instead they are built over time. We are constantly asking ourselves, 'What is this most like?' We look for patterns that we recognise from previous experiences to make meaning of our experiences and make predictions. They help us make sense of our experience in a quick and efficient way.

The idea that we can change the very structure of the brain is still pretty new, but over the last decade the advances in our understanding of brain malleability (or neuroplasticity) have shown that we are constantly creating, recreating and reinforcing patterns. These might be thoughts, feelings or behaviours, but when we repeatedly trigger these patterns, they form nerve (neuron) clusters which fire together, and as neuroscientists say, 'the cells that fire together, wire together'.

When we learn any new skill, like playing the piano for example, the areas associated with learning this new skill rapidly grow more nerve connections, creating denser, thicker brain tissue in that area. It's a bit like developing muscle tissue through regular repetition.

The good news is that, by the same token, the less we repeat those patterns the weaker they become. So we can change our thoughts, feelings and behaviours by creating new patterns — patterns of thinking, feeling or behaving.

Rapid 'Pattern Interrupt' techniques

These exercises will instantly interrupt your anxious thinking pattern:

Bilateral Stimulation. When you're in the grip of anxiety (or any other strong emotion) a particular part of your brain will be over-stimulated, leading to an imbalance in activity between the two sides of your brain. The idea of this exercise is to stimulate both hemispheres in order to even out the electrical activity across the brain and calm it down. It's amazingly simple but really does work. To try it out, find an object such as a bottle, or ball which you can easily pass from hand to hand. Now think of something that makes you feel anxious. Once you can really feel that, start passing the bottle from hand to hand across the front of your body, swinging out to each side and then swapping over again at about the mid-point. Slow it down and make it more rhythmic; you could say 'left' and right' as you do that. If you do this for 30 secs to one minute, you will notice the anxiety has reduced considerably.

Peripheral Vision. This is another very quick way of shifting your mental state. Start by finding a spot on the wall or other point and fix your focus on it. Notice the colour, texture and so on, and then whilst still looking at that spot, defocus your eyes and become aware of your peripheral vision, in other words the areas to the left and right of your field of vision. You can extend that to imagining the space behind you. You'll notice your jaw relaxing... and a few moments of this will really reduce tension. Repeat a few times and this will quickly calm your nervous system and help move your focus outside yourself when your inner voice is bothersome. Author Carlos Castaneda calls this 'stopping the world'.

Hand tracing. This calming exercise involves simply tracing your fingers. First relax your shoulders. Now hold one hand up in front of you, facing you, fingers fanned out. With the other hand slowly and mindfully trace up and down each finger, and then back again. Follow the movement with your eyes and as you move up and down, gently breathe in and out. Repeat a few times and then spend a few moments just simply becoming aware of the space between your fingers. It's the defocus idea again.

Heart coherence breathing. This is one of my favourites. It's a technique based on the work of the HeartMath Institute. Try it now. Put your hand on the area of your heart in the centre of your chest. Shift your focus to that area, perhaps close your eyes, and allow your breath to slowly flow in and out of that area, make it slower and deeper. Then actively focus on creating a warm positive feeling, such as compassion or appreciation, perhaps by thinking of someone you care for — I usually think of my dog — it's always so easy to access feelings for a pet you love! Allow your face to soften and notice an inner smile. Continue with this feeling as you begin to notice that all stress has just melted away. This technique allows you to connect with your intuitive intelligence and creates a state of coherence with your inner self. It really does feel good.

'Breath is the essence of life. We breathe to stay alive, to nourish the cells and organs of the body, and we breathe as a gesture of hope. It is the doorway to the next moment, and from that the next possible future.' MARIA SIROIS

Chapter 5
Changing your Internal Landscape

> *'Worry is a thin stream of fear trickling through the mind. If encouraged, it cuts a channel into which all other thoughts are drained.'* ARTHUR SOMERS ROCHE

Is it safe to assume then, that having got this far in the book you've decided it's time to change? That you'd like to teach your Good Girl to stay in the background, so you can live your life free from the self-imposed limitations you have been tolerating up to now? Just to recap then, I'd like you to answer the questions below, because if you are to put in the effort needed, it's important to remind yourself <u>why</u> you want to do it:

- Have you identified the probable origins of your Good Girl?

- Are you clear about why you want to change, about the benefits?

- And what will be different when you have begun to make those changes?

Good Wolf, Bad Wolf

So how do we begin to loosen the grip of the anxiety caused by allowing our Good Girl to be in charge? The first step is self-awareness. It's important to recognise what triggers your anxiety, to identify what makes it worse or better and understand the habits that 'feed' it.

I love the old Cherokee legend known as the 'Tale of the Two Wolves'. A grandfather explains to his warrior grandson that there are two wolves within each of us: the good wolf is positive and beneficial — he is joy, peace, love, hope, serenity, humility, kindness, benevolence, empathy, generosity, truth, compassion, and faith. On the other hand, the bad wolf is negative and destructive — he is anger, envy, sorrow, regret, greed, arrogance, self-pity, guilt, resentment, inferiority, lies, false pride, superiority, and ego. These two wolves fight for control over us. The grandson is curious and asks, 'But Grandfather, which wolf will win?', and the grandfather replies, 'The one that wins is the one you feed the most.'

So how can you ensure that you feed the good wolf and not the bad wolf?

Changing your anxious thinking

From the moment you were born you began to develop your attitudes and beliefs about yourself, about others and the world around you. Your parents, other family members and so on all influenced this development, and because you were too young to question them, you unconsciously accepted their ideas as if they were your own.

You have created an image of yourself based on the opinions of other people, or what you <u>perceived</u> those opinions to be. Think back — as you grew up were you labelled in some way? Perhaps you were 'the quiet one', 'the clever one', 'pretty' or 'helpful'. Or the 'problem one', the 'fussy one', 'sensitive' or 'slow'? These deeply ingrained beliefs about ourselves can stay with us.

As we go through life we continue to create our image of

ourselves, effortlessly nourishing and reinforcing those beliefs, and behaving in a way that fits with that image. It's almost as if we're blinkered and can only see ourselves this way. Unconsciously we look for evidence to support and feed those limiting beliefs, and we often ignore evidence to the contrary — which if we noticed it, would show us how ridiculous, unfair and unhelpful those beliefs really are!

Your Inner Critic

I'm sure you know what I mean when I talk about that little gremlin that sits on your shoulder and whispers in your ear — 'you'd be useless at that', 'they don't really want you in the team', or 'he thinks you're an idiot'. These self-defeating and self-critical thoughts create anxiety, guilt, shame and anger. They affect your self-confidence, limit your ability to deal with difficulties in life, and often stop you from achieving your goals.

That 'Inner Critic' is very insidious and quite toxic, and it fans the flames of shame. It begins quietly and before you know it, it's like the loudest voice in the room. So why is it there? Its purpose is to keep you safe, to protect you. It makes perfect sense when you think about it. It's the job of the primitive part of your brain to prevent you from doing anything to threaten your survival, so it urges you to be cautious. But, of course, we are not in mortal danger very often, so the message is really an 'error' message. Why not take a moment to list as many of your self-critical thoughts as you can in the box below. Getting those thoughts out from where they lurk gives you the chance to see them for what they really are!

Our thoughts directly affect our feelings and consequently our behaviour, so it's very important to think in positive terms about yourself and your life. This is one of the most important lessons you can learn, and understanding that this choice is yours, and yours alone, can change your life forever. It's like your own 'light bulb moment'.

When you feel anxious, try to become aware of your negative thoughts and then challenge them. Are they fair, rational, TRUE? I bet they don't stand up to scrutiny. Basically, these are negative 'instructions' you're giving to your subconscious! Now why would you willingly do that? So what are your most regularly played negative thoughts? In other words, what are you feeding the bad wolf?

My Self-Critical Thoughts:

Other Negative Thoughts:

Writing them down is a good first step to taking an objective look at them. Are they true, logical, helpful? If not, what would be a more realistic, more positive thought? This will help to dissipate those unhelpful irrational beliefs rather than reinforcing them.

Basically, the more rigid your beliefs, the more rules-driven you are, the more stress and anxiety you will feel. Look out for thoughts like 'should', 'must', 'have to', 'ought to'. When you catch yourself thinking 'I should' — ask 'who said so?' What's the worst that can happen if you <u>don't</u> do this, whatever it is. Then it's your choice. When you think a 'should' you instantly feel tired, you feel flat. Try changing it to a 'want to' or even a 'need to' — both of which produce more energy.

The ability to make our own choices is a very strong and empowering belief and leads you to feel more in control of your life.

Think again. Those old, outdated self-defeating thoughts will resurface every now and again — but you will gradually get better at ignoring them. So please don't become discouraged. It's about changing old habits, and that takes time! Try having some favourite coping statements ready — such as 'so what?', 'who cares?', 'does it really matter?', 'I don't think like that anymore', 'I'm fine whatever happens' — anything that works for you. If something is boring, try: 'it's tedious, but I can handle it.' Or: 'I feel a bit nervous, but that's okay!' We all have negative thoughts, <u>but just because you think it, does NOT make it true</u>. Much of what we think is irrational and pretty unhelpful!

If you do a lot of **'awfulising'** or think in **'catastrophic'** terms, this will make everything appear worse than it really is. Take a moment to consider how often you over-react by thinking, or saying that something is 'terrible', 'horrendous', 'a nightmare', 'a disaster'. How often is something SO bad? Is the world going to end or the sky fall in? So resolve to <u>notice</u> what you are thinking, challenge the rationality of it and decide how you might **change** it. It takes practice but honestly, it's worth it. Over time you will find yourself feeling more calm, less emotional and more able to see things in perspective.

Another way of changing our thinking is to try looking at

things in a different way, called 'reframing'. If we mentally stand back and ask ourselves what's another, more rational way of seeing this situation, or how might someone else view it, it can help us see things more clearly.

Resilience is about keeping going even when things are difficult or frustrating. It's about noticing when you tell yourself 'I can't stand this' or 'I can't cope with that'. Is it really 'awful' or 'dreadful'? The truth is, you don't always have to feel comfortable, and yes, **you can stand it**!

Which of the following 'thinking distortions' do you recognise in your own thinking?

☐ Jumping to conclusions

☐ Mind reading

☐ Seeing things only from my point of view

☐ Thinking in 'all-or-nothing' terms

☐ Thinking in a demanding way about myself or others — 'musts', 'shoulds', 'have to's'

☐ Totally condemning myself or others because of one mistake

☐ Blaming myself for something that isn't really (or entirely) my fault

☐ Blowing things up out of proportion

☐ Expecting myself or others to be perfect

☐ Labelling myself or others ('he's just a loser', 'I'm really stupid', etc)

☐ Just seeing the negative side of things (discounting the positives)

☐ Fretting about how things should be instead of accepting and dealing with the reality

☐ Fortune-telling — believing we can see into the future, expecting things to turn out badly

☐ Assuming I can't do anything to change the situation

☐ Concentrating on my weaknesses and ignoring my strengths

If you're a Good Girl, you probably ticked quite a few of those. I wonder how often you jump to conclusions or make assumptions about what people are thinking about you? So common with Good Girls.

> *'Our greatest freedom is the freedom to choose our attitude.'*
> VIKTOR FRANKL, Holocaust survivor

Thought Stopping

When you find yourself feeling unhappy or anxious, take a moment to look at what's going on in your head. What are you thinking or imagining? You could think of excessive worrying as if it were a fairground merry-go-round, one with colourful horses going up and down. Sometimes those thoughts are going around so fast that we hardly know what they really are. It's like one big blur of worry! When that happens, there are two things you can try:

• Just imagine you are slowing that merry-go-round right down to a stop. Slowly the individual worries come into focus and are clearly identifiable. Then you can use some problem-solving skills. Look at each one and ask yourself what (if anything) you can do about them. Are they rational thoughts or can you tell yourself something more helpful? Perhaps there is something practical you can do about this 'worry'? Get tough on worrying!

• Simply firmly telling yourself 'STOP' can work really well. If you're in a room full of people, probably best said to yourself (!), but it's very effective if you *can* say it out loud! It sometimes helps to imagine a 'stop' sign, or traffic lights or a big neon sign — whatever works for you. It's simple, but I use it myself quite often — I like simple ideas.

Pattern matching

When you experience anything in life, your brain tries to make sense of it by matching it to something similar in the past, to give you the right emotional response (leading you to take the most appropriate action). We call this a 'pattern matching'. Think back to early man. Imagine the scene. He is foraging for food and sees some red berries. Immediately his brain looks for a similar experience in the past. If he had a bad stomach ache after eating red berries the last time he picked them, he won't want to make the same mistake again.

It's about survival.

At a very basic level, for example, a new-born baby will pattern match a nipple to the instinct of suckling — this is a good pattern match, but sucking Mum's finger is a faulty pattern match. So how useful or appropriate this match is will correspond with how mentally healthy we are. We have a powerful imagination, so you can see why it's easy to develop faulty pattern matches.

Let's imagine that you have been asked to give a presentation at a large meeting next Thursday. You know it's important for your career, but you really hate having to speak in public. Although you've done it before there's a good chance you will 'pattern match' to an unpleasant memory or imagery of giving a presentation. Even if previous talks have gone perfectly well, perhaps you suffered terrible anxiety in the lead up and continued to feel stressed throughout the event.

This is the image you see: your mouth is dry and your face flushed, you look and feel embarrassed and self-conscious, they weren't listening or interested, you fear you will lose your thread and look like an idiot. This is a powerful (if exaggerated) memory. So you automatically imagine that previous time, become flooded with anxiety and then every time you think about 'next Thursday' you experience that same feeling of dread.

> '*Our lives are like movies: we have to edit them to create a coherent story. But sometimes we need to go back to unused footage to find material for a better version. A better version of ourselves.*'
> Positive Psychologist MARGARITA TARRAGONA

Why do we remember the negative experiences more easily? Again, it's about our mind keeping us safe, it wants to protect us and when we trigger anxiety and stress, our brain interprets that to mean we are in danger and the emotion created is powerful. We tend not to pattern match back to the good experiences because they are just an extra bonus, the vital thing apparently is to stay safe.

Focusing on the negative is an ancient survival mechanism, but in the modern age it is a burden that holds us back. So next time you have an anxiety attack or feel panicky, think of it as a 'protection' attack instead. Think of it as an outdated error message which by ignoring, you can delete.

It's an interesting fact that when we are depressed, we focus more on negative memories and dissociate from positive ones. For example, we remember our childhood more negatively when feeling low, whereas when things are going well, we remember our childhood as being happier. So when you begin to feel negative, do something to change your mood. Take a solution-focused approach. Think about what works for you.

Your personal reality tunnel

So we each have our own version of reality, we live in our own 'reality tunnel'. We share experiences with others and somehow believe we are in the same reality. Yet the truth is we are conditioned from birth. We see everything through our own filters, created from childhood and added to as we go through life. We tend to notice things that re-enforce our beliefs and expectations but ignore things that don't. This is how we build our filters, one on top of the other, thereby creating our own totally individual reality.

> *'Reality is merely an illusion, albeit a very persistent one.'*
> EINSTEIN

In order to keep things in perspective, we need to regularly step outside ourselves and try to see things from a different point of view. It helps us to understand and empathise with others more readily, and also to realise that we all struggle with difficulties and obstacles that don't really exist, except in our own heads.

We are **'meaning-making machines'**. Without even realising it, at an unconscious level we are constantly interpreting the world around us, the things that happen to us and the things people say and do. When someone ignores you or is rude, your mind makes its own meaning out of it, based on your inner beliefs and attitudes. And it's completely automatic — in other words you don't stop and give it any thought — it happens without any effort on your part.

The meanings you make affect the way you feel, and then how you behave as a result. So the interpretations you make about the things that happen in life have a significant influence on the amount of anxiety you experience in your day.

It pays us to remember that there are many versions of the 'truth'.

Magical thinking and obsession

Good Girls often have a lot of 'free floating' anxiety, which allows fear to attach itself to many different aspects of life. It can lead to obsessive thinking and even progress to become obsessive compulsive disorder (OCD) — a bit like having a relentless slavedriver inside your head. We are prone to 'magical thinking' too, perhaps imagining that we can cause or avert disasters, for example thinking 'if I sit at the back of the plane, it will crash'.

These usually begin in childhood, like the idea that if we tread on the cracks in the pavement something terrible will happen! If we make a habit of indulging in this type of thinking, then patterns become set as habits, and these take some effort to break. So start by noticing your magical thinking. What messages are you giving to your unconscious mind — and how you are 'doing' anxiety?

The Power of Your Imagination

It's not only your thoughts that matter. You are constantly creating your internal landscape by what you think AND what you imagine all day long. Most of us have no idea how powerful our imagination really is — and it's all too easy to get into the habit of running a background film packed with negative suggestions and negative images. It goes without saying that's bound to affect almost every aspect of life.

Do you sometimes find yourself daydreaming, or so absorbed in something that you don't notice what's going on around you — you might even lose track of time? Actually, whenever you're focusing inwards and deeply absorbed it's a similar psychological state to hypnosis. So this is very natural to us; in fact, we are in this light hypnotic state many times during the day. And, if you can use it negatively, it stands to reason you can use it positively too.

What we focus on we get more of, <u>so focus on what you want, not what you don't want</u>.

Let's say you're at work; do you feel anxious when faced with people of higher status than you — more experienced, more knowledgeable, more authoritative? I bet you do — it's a very typical Good Girl thing. Think about a time when you were in a situation like this — perhaps it was an interview, a work meeting or a presentation you had to give. I'm betting you thought about it a great deal beforehand, running that mental imagery of how you expected it to be. Just take a few moments now to remember such a time. Try to recall the imagery you were creating whilst anticipating the upcoming event. Did you imagine yourself as small and insignificant, perhaps blushing, looking uncomfortable, saying something stupid or not knowing what you 'should' know? Perhaps you imagined the more 'important' person as bigger, unfriendly, looking down on you, not interested in your ideas...? Everything is exaggerated and cartoon-like, as you see it from your own strangely skewed perspective.

This is something most of us do, not just you. We mentally

rehearse future events which we are worried about, and our imagination takes over. In its attempts to protect us, our unconscious mind makes everything scarier and more negative in almost every way! Its job is to ensure we survive and if we are to make it to tomorrow, let's avoid any challenges, avoid doing anything different and at least we have a chance!

But it's an error message — after all, what's the worst that can happen if you make a mistake or look foolish? Chances are no-one will even notice (except you) and if they do, they will have forgotten it in a day or two. The truth is that most people are far too busy thinking about themselves to care about your shortcomings! They're worrying about what they look like, if they're clever enough, interesting enough, popular enough, funny enough — just like you.

Exactly the same happens when we re-run unpleasant memories. The angry face of your partner becomes more furious, the throw-away comment your friend made feels like a knife in your heart, and your minor mistake has grown into a feeling of gut-wrenching shame. Be careful what imagery you allow to run in your mind — when we focus on painful traumatic memories, we experience the bad feelings all over again. In fact, every time we re-run a memory we change it slightly, because we are viewing it through the magnifying glass of our own unique perspective. So it won't be a true and accurate representation of what actually happened at all.

This is important — you can use your imagination more productively. Focus more on visualising what you want instead of running that old unhelpful film. See yourself performing confidently, being relaxed, telling yourself it's fine. Imagine the others smiling and listening to you with interest. They are only people like you, and they weren't always so knowledgeable and experienced! Imagine it going the way you want it to. Similarly, we can change our painful memories, but more about that later.

Visualisation Exercises

At the end of each of the remaining chapters I'm going to take you through a visualisation exercise. This will help you learn how to really harness the power of your imagination and rehearse making the changes want to make. If you'd prefer to, why not record them and listen instead. Or you could play some music as you visualise, but choose your music carefully so that it will truly enhance the experience.

It might feel a bit unnatural at first, but it isn't complicated, and you will find it easier and easier the more you practise.

Read it through a few times so that you can do it without stopping.

VISUALISATION

Relax and focus inwards (this first part will be the same for each of the visualisations)

Find somewhere quiet — *sit or lie down. Make yourself comfortable and close your eyes. Now...take a few lovely, deep cleansing breaths.... in through your nose and out through your mouth. As you breathe out...feel your mind clearing and feel your shoulders relaxing.*

Now breathing nice and easily...every time you breathe out, say to yourself *'relax now'*, relax your shoulders a little more and allow that feeling to flow down through your body, relaxing every muscle, every fibre, every cell. Your unconscious can allow your body to relax...

Feel yourself drifting deeper into relaxation. Some people like the idea of slowly sinking into warm water, others lying on a warm beach, or walking in a beautiful forest; whatever enhances the relaxation for you. If you have intrusive thoughts, just let them come and go, like clouds moving across the sky. As you focus inwards you allow the deeper part of your mind to help you make the changes you want to make.

Creating a More Positive Image of Yourself

Visualise yourself in your wonderfully relaxing place. It might be somewhere you've been, or you can create somewhere from your imagination. Add in vibrant colours, sounds and smells that please you, like the smell of strawberries or newly cut grass. Smell in particular is a very powerful 'anchor' to feelings, both positive and negative. Really feel the good feelings and bring this mental film to life.

Now I want you to see yourself in various situations where you would like to feel more relaxed, happy and confident. You're going to take some time to build the positive imagery in your mind, adding in the detail, and then mentally rehearse it as if running a film.

Imagine sending new instructions to your subconscious mind...the more you do that the more possibilities and ideas will come to you.

See yourself making these changes, getting into the right mindset, trusting yourself to respond differently...and allowing *this new version of yourself to grow. You're thinking more positively, overcoming difficulties, feeling positive and confident, sensing an upsurge of positive energy and desire for change.*

Gently bring yourself back to normal awareness, and back to your day, feeling energised. Confident that you are now releasing yourself from the influence of your Good Girl.

Chapter 6
Self-compassion

'*Love yourself... enough to take the actions required for your happiness...enough to cut yourself loose from the drama-filled past... enough to set a high standard for relationships... enough to feed your mind and body in a healthy manner... enough to forgive yourself... enough to move on.*' STEVE MARABOLI, Unapologetically You: Reflections on Life and the Human Experience

As a Good Girl, being kind and compassionate to yourself is likely to be an unfamiliar concept. You may be well versed in being empathic and thinking of others, but be honest, when it comes to self-compassion you are much more familiar with self-criticism and beating yourself up. It isn't something that came easily to me, I must admit. Throughout time women have always understood the need for duty, responsibility and looking after others, but the idea of loving yourself? To a Good Girl that sounds a lot like self-indulgence and selfishness!

I can only imagine what the women of years gone by would have made of the idea of looking after yourself as a priority. Yet here we are in the 21st century and things haven't changed nearly enough. Still we have to almost actively give ourselves permission to care for us. If we don't invest in our own well-being, then who will? We need to nurture ourselves, experience feelings of compassion within us; otherwise we can't truly give it to others. In order to be healthy and well, mentally and physically, we cannot ignore our own needs.

So make a decision now to be kinder to yourself, to cut yourself some slack. We shape our lives by making small changes every day, so why not start a new habit today, of accepting yourself just as you are, with all your qualities, negative and positive. You are a fallible human being, just like the rest of us, doing your best to get by in a complex world.

Earlier I talked about the neurotransmitter oxytocin, the 'love hormone', and how beneficial it is to your well-being as an antidote to anxiety. Here is an exercise which will produce feelings of compassion within you. It will increase levels of oxytocin (along with other hormones), and quickly make you feel more relaxed with a greater sense of well-being.

How to increase your oxytocin

1. Sit or lie down. Relax into the space around you and allow your breathing to deepen, use the exhalation to relax you. Close your eyes.

2. Imagine a warmth developing in the centre of your chest, around the area of your heart. This represents self-love or compassion. What colour is that feeling? Really connect with that feeling and enjoy the sense of unconditional love for yourself.

3. Now allow it to flow to all parts of your body…and even beyond. Allow an 'inner smile' as you feel a sense of connection to your fellow man, the world around you and the universe beyond.

This exercise can take just a few moments or longer if you have time. Either way you will notice an instant benefit. Try it for yourself. Remember that in order to feel compassion and love for others, we must first love and care for ourselves.

> *'Love is a state of being. Your love is not outside; it is deep within you. You cannot lose it, and it will never leave you.'*
> ECKHART TOLLE

Taking care of yourself is your responsibility and must be your priority. No-one else can do that for you and loving and accepting yourself is the first step. When you give yourself the gift of unconditional love and self-respect, others will pick up on that…. and treat you differently.

So you see, we show others how to treat us.

Healing your Inner Child (to combat shame)

One of the most powerful unconscious influences on each of us is our Inner Child. Whatever age you are, there is a little child inside you. She is at the core of your being, your 'feeling' self. She can be creative, joyful and playful; however, the other side of this Inner Child is vulnerable, sensitive and insecure. We all know what it's like to feel that vulnerability, to feel fragile and lonely at times, but if you experienced fear or harsh treatment in your childhood, your Inner Child will be especially wounded. You could think of her as an earlier version of your Good Girl.

This Wounded Child lives on in the adult body, fending for herself in a grown-up world and controlling us at a subconscious level. An overly compliant Inner Child can make us feel anxious about doing and saying the wrong thing. We don't like breaking rules and can become highly self-critical. No wonder we repress our feelings and feel insecure. We can become hurt and angry, needy, dependent, fearful of abandonment.

There are times for all of us when we need tender loving care, just as a child would, and rather than locking away painful feelings and stifling them, instead we must acknowledge and feel them. Feelings have energy and even if we try to suppress them, the emotional impact doesn't go away. It stays around, beneath the surface and instead shows up as anxiety, depression, physical pain, addiction and so on.

As adults we often search for others to rescue us from our insecurity and self-doubt, to make us feel more loved and cared for. But they can't do that; we must learn to do that for ourselves. Being grown up means you are no longer dependent and helpless, you have a choice about how much you accept and how you respond. You can't change the past, but you can gain comfort and relief by 'reparenting' your Inner Child; learning to love and nurture yourself.

So how can you begin to heal your Inner Child?

1. Sit quietly and relax. Visualise yourself in a relaxing place and imagine meeting your child self. You might find it easier if you think of somewhere you remember as a child, your home, the dinner table, school or playground. Allow it to come to your mind; it doesn't matter if it isn't very clear. Make friends with that little girl inside. Listen, what does she need? Love, acceptance, protection, understanding...? Be compassionate, allow laughter and tears, answer her questions, hug her, and reach a new understanding. Tell her she is unconditionally loved as herself, that she is good enough. She can relax now because you'll always be there for her, to provide love, support and reassurance.

Whenever you feel upset, or negative feelings trigger your Good Girl (you might experience it as a physical sensation), please do try this exercise. At a deep level you will sense some healing; a greater feeling of unity and inner peace within you.

Then breathe and let the image fade.

2. You could also draw a picture of her — but with your non-dominant hand. Just let it happen, don't plan it, be patient. What was that like? How did it feel? What did the child seem to be saying? Keep a private notebook for your experiences. Perhaps write a letter to your younger self. Try visiting different ages of your childhood, and gradually you will feel a sense of reconciliation and understanding, and a new relationship will emerge.

3. How about finding a photograph of your younger self? You can choose a special frame and display it somewhere that feels right. Now whenever you feel your Vulnerable Inner Child being triggered you can send some love and comfort her way!

These exercises might make you feel emotional, but if you find yourself particularly upset by it please get some support. Perhaps you will decide to talk to a therapist.

Releasing Guilt

Earlier on I talked about shame and how it is usually the foundation upon which our Good Girl is built. But is guilt the same as shame? No, although if you often feel shame, you're probably more likely to feel guilt. Shame is more deeply internalised because it is often first experienced at a very young age. It is intensely painful, a feeling that we are somehow innately flawed, worthless or defective.

Guilt, however, is about something we have done, rather than something we <u>are</u>. It's a complex emotion and there's a big difference between 'healthy' guilt and 'unhealthy' guilt.

Let's say you've hurt someone's feelings or caused a problem which could have been avoided. You feel really bad, and recognising that you could have done it differently, regret what happened. Regret is a healthy response, but the real growth happens when you decide to accept what happened, learn from it and move on. That way, when you come face to face with a similar situation, you can choose to do things differently.

'Unhealthy' guilt relates to doing something that goes against your unrealistically high standards or imagined rules. Perhaps you forgot someone's name or inadvertently jumped a queue. These are not major transgressions but because of your interpretation you feel remorseful and terrible. 'Unhealthy' guilt can lead to self-blame and a feeling of being 'stuck' in the guilt.

I'm sure that you can think of times when you've acted in a way that triggers guilt. Typically, they would fit into these categories:

• Something you did (or think you did): I will never forget one time when we were living in Hong Kong — it's etched into my memory. I was at a party and stood chatting with a group of women, one of whom appeared to be pregnant, so I innocently congratulated her on it. You guessed it — she wasn't pregnant. Nevertheless, she passed it off graciously, saving my blushes just a little. The most devastating thing was that a month or two later I discovered that she was very ill with ovarian cancer. I was mortified.

• Something you didn't do: Perhaps you have a friend who relies on you for her emotional support. She tells you she knows you're always there for her and that she doesn't know what she'd do without you. However, recently, because you're not feeling at your best and this over-dependency is beginning to get you down, you haven't been answering her calls. You care about your friend, so you feel bad. It's not easy to know when to pull back or say 'No', but for me it's about giving from the heart, not out of guilt.

• The way you felt: For example, we might feel angry or frustrated with a child or elderly parent, even when we know we 'shouldn't' be.

• For needing help: Whether emotional support, practical help or just a bit of advice, it can be so difficult to admit we need help and feel really uncomfortable asking for it. It taps into our feelings of shame, makes us feel exposed and vulnerable.

• For having more than someone else: It could be guilt at being pregnant when your friend is unable to conceive or having more money or success than your sister.

• Something you didn't do well enough: You failed to meet your 'be perfect' standards at work and your team lost the contract.

Those are just a few examples; there are many more. In fact, we can feel guilty about almost anything! The key question to ask yourself is: 'Is it reasonable to feel guilty about this?' Are you beating yourself up over something that wasn't your fault, something that's just a normal human mistake, or an understandable emotion?

The likelihood is, though, that you're feeling guilty out of habit, a habit created by your inner Good Girl. What better time than this to stop feeling guilty about everything and everyone, and instead practise some self-compassion! Here are some ideas about how to do it. It takes time and patience but does get easier.

1. If you make a mistake, admit it. Say sorry, take

responsibility and accept that you're disappointed with yourself. You're human and we all make mistakes. Learn from it and forgive yourself. If you are going over and over it in your mind, re-living every last detail (and probably exaggerating it all), notice that. When we re-imagine painful or shameful memories, we strengthen them. Instead imagine it differently, see the past through a positive lens, from a different and more realistic perspective. Then be kind to yourself and let it go.

2. Notice the harsh voice of that inner critic — what are you telling yourself about what happened? Remember that your brain believes what you tell it, so choose a better thought. What would a good friend say to you right now? Be your own best friend. Show some compassion for that inner critic. She doesn't realise she's getting the job wrong.

3. Write it down. I'll talk more about journaling later, but there's something very powerful and cathartic about writing down your feelings. It gets it out there where you can see it and makes it easier to see what's real and what's imagined. You could perhaps have a conversation with that Inner Critic. It will help you identify unhelpful thought patterns and see how you are sabotaging yourself. In turn that makes it easier to be kind to yourself and practise self-forgiveness.

4. Take a breath. I know it sounds too simple — but simple is often the best. In her book *A Short Course in Happiness After Loss: (and Other Dark, Difficult Times)*, positive psychologist Maria Sirois talks about the breath being the essence of life, deeply nourishing and healing. It feeds us with life-giving energy, rejuvenates, renews and calms us. Whenever you feel upset, emotional and out of balance with the world, the breath is like a little oasis of calm, a transition from one state to another, mindfully taking you from one

moment to the next. It clears, dissolves and sets us free. Taking that breath is like a gift you give yourself.

If you ever meet a person who claims never to have felt guilty, be wary of them. Either they're just saying it for effect or if they're being real, it means they have very little empathy. If we feel a connection with others, if we can imagine their pain, sadness or disappointment, the bottom line is we will sometimes feel guilty. Stop being so hard on yourself — it's called being human.

Loving All Your Parts

If you can find a way of making peace with that inner critic, you are on the path to self-acceptance. And once on that path you are not so far from learning to love yourself — just as you are. We all have our 'dark side', those unlovable bits of ourselves, the angry, wounded, mean parts. But you are much, much more than those negative parts. They developed as a response to life's difficulties, to help you cope with pain and disappointment, and not feeling good enough. Their job was to protect you, to encourage you to get your needs met, but somewhere along the line the messages all became rather outdated.

See them for what they are; learn to embrace mistakes and those parts that you think of as weak or flawed, and recognise that you are like everyone else, yes, I do mean everyone else. You are the sum of many parts which make up one whole human being, perfectly imperfect!

It's helpful to befriend these negative parts, without judgement. By showing understanding and compassion to them, we can allow stronger connection to the more positive parts and create a better balance within. For example, it's okay to feel scared sometimes, because out of this can grow courage. It's okay to feel angry sometimes if it leads us to take action for change. In this way we can begin to acknowledge and integrate those parts.

When you are in the grip of any of those negative parts ask yourself: what's really going on here? And what do I need right now? Listening to your needs and working out what's right for you is like being your own best friend, showing respect and kindness to yourself.

Your Innate Wisdom

There is one part of us that is always aware of our changing emotional state, but which is <u>not</u> caught up in those emotions. It is the quiet wisdom at the centre of our being, our sense of wholeness, and independent of passing emotions. This wise part of us knows us very well, and we forget that we can access it at any time if we choose to tune in to it. Whatever is happening in your life, your wise self is objectively observing you, so try asking for advice and listening for the answer from within. You'll almost certainly get wise counsel!

There is no doubt that life will always have its ups and downs, successes and failures, joy and suffering. But please don't underestimate your ability to ride that rollercoaster, to embrace your experiences. Underneath your feelings of anxiety, insecurity and self-doubt there is so much more that you almost certainly aren't acknowledging, so much potential waiting to be nurtured. Like tender young saplings that can only flourish and bloom if you lovingly tend them. But that means deciding that you deserve to blossom! No more waiting until you feel 'good enough', it's time to love yourself right now, warts and all. No more excuses. Our connections to others are vital to our well-being, but if we don't have a loving acceptance and appreciation of ourselves, those outward connections are unable to root themselves securely. So hold yourself in a loving embrace, make your peace with the past and go forward bravely. Become your own hero.

This is how you plant the seeds of courage and create a new state of mind. As you begin to do things differently, speaking out more, stepping forward more, acting more positively, you

'In the midst of winter, I found there was within me an invincible summer.' ALBERT CAMUS

begin to see the benefits and do it more! That's positive re-enforcement and now you are truly creating a new way of thinking and behaving. How amazing is that?

So let's have a look at how you see yourself, because the image you have of yourself is bound to be miles away from a true reflection of who you are, and indeed how others see you.

EXERCISE: The Friendly Mirror

I believe this exercise was originally conceived by internationally renowned coach, Michael Neill, though it has been adapted and used by many others. It will help you shift your perspective.

1. Stand in front of a mirror (ideally a full length one) and close your eyes.

2. Think of a time when someone you respect or trust paid you a sincere compliment. Just accept that they meant what they said. You don't have to believe it!

3. Open your eyes and look in the mirror and imagine seeing yourself through THEIR eyes. See what they saw, notice what they noticed. Bearing in mind you may be so used to seeing yourself negatively, from your own skewed perspective, this might be hard for you. If that's so, then just focus on your eyes as you look in the mirror, as that will help stop you getting caught up in self-criticism.

4. Send love and approval to the you in the mirror. Feel that compassion, that warmth around your heart. Think of someone you love until you can feel those wonderful feelings welling up in your body. Then open your eyes and allow yourself to accept them — they are for you. Notice any difference. Perhaps you have a more relaxed and confident look about you. Is there a subtle change in the way you hold yourself or move? Has the way you think about yourself shifted just a little?

5. Finally imagine taking a mental snapshot of this more authentic you that you now see in the mirror. Any time you want to you can revisit that image, seeing your reflection through the eyes of love, and feel those good feelings all over again. Slowly you are reprogramming your subconscious to see yourself in a more positive, more kindly way.

Try this. Right now I'd like you to write down <u>three things</u> <u>you deeply appreciate about yourself</u>:

Support

We all need support from our fellow human beings and yet it often seems difficult to ask for it. I admit I find it so. I think those years at school away from my family meant I learnt to be overly self-reliant, which can make it difficult to know when you need help, and even more challenging to ask for it.

Being a Good Girl means we are usually much more aware of pleasing others than admitting we need help. We don't want to be any trouble, and often worry about being in someone's debt too. Then there's our pride — we don't want to admit we're struggling. Let's just feel hard done by, and feel like a martyr then, shall we?

The truth is it's a good idea to have a few people we can rely on when in need. Have a think about your support system, and who you can talk to, depending on what you need at that particular moment. The person you can rely on in a crisis might not be the same person who will be honest about how overly sensitive you're being.

Write a name beside each of these:

- Someone I can rely on in a crisis...
- Someone who helps me feel good about myself...
- Someone I can be totally myself with...
- Someone who will be really honest with me...
- Someone I can talk to if I'm worried...
- Someone who really makes me stop and think about what I'm doing...
- Someone who is lively to be with...
- Someone who introduces me to new ideas, new interests, new people...
- Someone who motivates and inspires me to take action...

If you've put the same one or two names down for all of them, then maybe it's time to broaden your support system. We need a mixture of people who can provide us with support in the different areas of our lives. The person we go to for motivation may not be the best listener.

The Surprising Power of Gratitude

When we focus our attention on what's wrong with our life, on what we're missing out on or what happened in the past, we forget to be grateful for what we have. We are so much in the habit of comparing our lives with those who appear 'luckier', more fortunate or just plain happier that it's all too easy to feel like victims. How often do you consider the little things that bring you joy? The truth is, joy so often comes in ordinary moments and it's so easy to forget how much in life can bring us pleasure, and to take what we have for granted.

Even when life is challenging, disappointing or painful you can still be grateful — for your home, a good friend, your pet, a lovely sunny day, beautiful music or the sound of children playing. Gratitude seems to open us up, to expand us. It's not an intellectual thing, it's a feeling — creating a moment of peace or contentment. And the more you do it the more you foster a positive attitude towards life, you become a receiver of good things, and the more you notice them, the more you receive them.

Brené Brown talks about 'softening into joy'. It can make us feels vulnerable, but in fact these moments give us warmth, strength and help build resilience. Brené's young daughter apparently used to describe these as 'picture memories' — she explained that she looked at them when she was feeling sad or lonely. The wisdom of innocence.

Strangely enough, it's often those who have had to cope with real loss or trauma who have most learnt to appreciate the joys, big and small, that life brings us.

So if you can develop the habit of celebrating the positives in this way, perhaps by keeping a gratitude journal and writing in it every day, you can really change how you experience your life. You will focus more on what you have as opposed to what you lack.

Priority No 1 — Taking Care of You

What would you be doing differently if you were really taking care of yourself? You may be going to the gym, eating healthily, but do you put enough time aside for enjoyment? I know how easy it is to find life that is so full of commitments that there is no time for pleasure. If this is you, then take a moment to stand back and think about your priorities. It's your responsibility to look after yourself — no-one is going to do that for you. Practising self-care and embracing pleasure are important if you are to keep yourself in a balanced healthy state of mind. It's simply not an option to keep your nose permanently attached to the grindstone or doing what you think others expect of you. Take a moment to consider this question: does your exaggerated sense of responsibility for what you <u>should</u> be doing mean you've shut yourself off from experiencing a lightness of being, joy, laughter?

'The amount of happiness that you have depends on the amount of freedom you have in your heart.' THICH NHAT HANH

These positive feelings release you from your Good Girl. You aren't judging or competing, worrying or striving to please. So what could you include in your life that would do that for you? It might be seeing more of your family or particular friends, going ice-skating, joining a choir, getting out in the garden, painting...the list is endless.

But remember, it's important that you don't approach the idea of having fun as something you 'should' be good at; otherwise it becomes something else. In fact, why not take a risk and try something you always fancied doing but doubted you'd be good at? How liberating that would be, to happily accept and indeed enjoy being mediocre (or no good) at something.

When you can give up the notion that everything you do is somehow a reflection of your personal worth, you can detach from the outcome and your world magically opens up. You might even start something and not need to finish it. How does your Good Girl feel about that! You can tell her, in no uncertain terms, that fun can just be fun — no judgement allowed!

Start writing a list of things that give you pleasure and add to it as you find more. It's similar to your gratitude list, but this time focusing on the pleasure principle. Tune into your senses to recall smells like clean laundry blowing in the breeze, or honeysuckle; or think about colours that you love, like the blue sky on a summer's day; sounds that give you joy, like the blackbird whose beautiful full-throated evening song makes you smile. It can be simple joys like these or going on an exciting trip with your family. This list is personal to you, and I think it will prove a pleasurable experience just writing it!

VISUALISATION

Begin with the 'Relax and Focus Inwards' section as you did at the end of Chapter 5, i.e. finding a quiet place, using your breathing and some beautiful imagery to allow you to deepen your relaxation and drift into a feeling of comfortable relaxing, then: continue with this session's visualisation.

Meeting Your Nurturing Self

Then, as you focus your mind inwards, take a few moments to allow an image to arise from the kindest, most loving part of yourself — this is the image of your nurturing self. Allow that image to become clearer... the colours, sounds and smells. What is she wearing? Perhaps she reminds you of someone? She might appear as a fairy, an angel or a classically motherly figure — in fact, anything at all that comes up for you. If an image doesn't arise easily, don't worry, just having a sense of her is fine. Feel her compassion and desire to help you towards a deeper understanding of yourself — of self-love and what that can mean for you. Welcome her, feel her kindness — perhaps a hug feels right. Tell her what you need and how she can help. You can share whatever you want to...and listen to whatever words of wisdom and comfort come from your subconscious. Allow her to help you be less critical, more accepting and more loving towards yourself, letting go of guilt and connecting with your innate wisdom.

If that nurturing part of you had a gift for you, what would it be? Allow your unconscious mind to come up with that gift, whatever it might be. Know that whenever you want her, she is there for you. Now gently bring yourself back to normal awareness, and back to your day, confident that you are releasing yourself from the influence of that Good Girl inside.

Chapter 7
Becoming Authentic

'*This above all: to thine own self be true,*
And it must follow, as the night the day,
Thou canst not be false to any man.'
WILLIAM SHAKESPEARE

What does it actually mean to be authentic? No-one else can judge what is at the heart of you; you have to work that out for yourself — what it means to be you. As far as we know this is your one life, your one chance to forge your own path and one chance to create your own story going forward. Who you are and what you do need to be aligned, if you are to live authentically. That means being aware when you are tempted to go along with the choices of others or noticing when you hold back because of fear. Be honest with yourself... then be brave.

Will the Real Me Step Forward?

Have you ever had one of those weird moments when just for a moment you question, 'Who am I...really?' I'm sure we all have. The truth is that none of us really knows the answer to that. But this is no time for a discussion about the meaning of consciousness, so let's stick with the notion of authenticity.

As we go through life we take on many different roles, and each of those brings into focus different aspects of the core self. We don't remain static, far from it, we change and grow all the time, exploring and developing parts of our identity at various stages in life. The choices we make, and whether or not we nurture our abilities, talents, relationships — as well as our circumstances — will all have a bearing on who we become.

Sometimes we feel we have to play a part or take on a role which feels quite a stretch from our real self, so much so that it seems fake and somehow 'wrong'.

Sometimes we get stuck and over-identify with one aspect of our lives — we all know those workaholics who seem to put all their energy into their jobs and have little time for anything else.

Thinking about the idea of identity reminds me of Helen. She ran her own insurance company and for her, work was all-consuming. She drove herself relentlessly, and as a result she felt overwhelmed and stressed. It was clear to me that so much of what she did was dictated by her Good Girl — the long hours at work, transporting her aging parents everywhere, supporting her sister financially, shopping for her neighbour; there simply wasn't enough of her to go around and she was finally discovering she wasn't superwoman after all. When I asked her about her interests outside work, what she did to relax, what brought her pleasure and so on, the truth began to dawn on her. Actually, it was only her work that seemed to bring enough meaning. It produced results she could measure, and on some level, she believed that if she worked hard enough, she would eventually feel she had met her high standards of achievement. You see, like many Good Girls she was still trying to prove herself.

Approaching retirement meant some difficult choices ahead and when I asked how that felt, she was quiet for a few moments and said, 'I don't know who I am without my work.' Another lightbulb moment for Helen. I'm pleased to say she has now retired, and she and her husband are very happy doing up an old cottage.

What's important is that as a general rule, whether at home, at work or with our friends we are still essentially the same person. The truth is that the more 'congruent' we are the less stress and anxiety we will experience. In other words, the less difference between our 'real' self and our 'revealed' self, the more we connect with and accept our true self. Let me ask you a question. Do we know when someone is being inauthentic? I believe we do — even if we often choose not to pay attention to the instinct that tells us so.

EXERCISE: The Real Me

Take a sheet of paper and draw a circle. That circle represents the 'you' that you show to the world. Now draw a second circle inside the first — this circle will represent your true self, the 'real' you. Notice the difference between the two. That's the 'you' that you keep secret, that consciously or deliberately you don't share. Perhaps it's the 'you' that you think you should be.

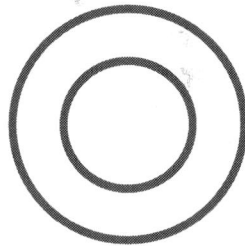

The 'real' me and the 'shown' me

To be clear, I'm not suggesting you need to tell your work colleagues everything about your life; that's not what being authentic means. It's about being straight, honest and free from the crippling fear of disapproval. It's about being able to relax as yourself, accepting who you are, and allowing yourself to be vulnerable sometimes. It's about letting your light shine through. Brené Brown says 'vulnerability is where fear and courage meet', which I think is a wonderful way of describing it. Once you are able to do this you can grow fully into yourself and move beyond the influence of your Good Girl.

The discomfort we feel when we have the inauthentic mask on tells us that we aren't being true to ourselves and whilst the reality is that we all have to 'fake it' sometimes, if we do it too much, or take it too far, we can begin to lose touch with our true self. And that will have a psychological price attached to it.

So think about it. Do you perhaps need to bring those two circles closer together to be more 'congruent' and how can you begin to do that? Perhaps you're like a 'square peg in a round hole' and need to make some significant changes, or perhaps just being a little more open with others will make a positive difference.

Your Values

One of the ways we can try to find out more about who we are and what truly matters to us is to identify our values, something you may not have given much thought to before. We each have a unique set of values that originate early in life and are based on the beliefs and attitudes of those around us, mainly our parents or carers. These guide our behaviour and our relationships with others and, in fact, change very little throughout our lives.

Your values represent your individual self, and when you

live in accordance with them, you're being true to yourself. They have deep emotional significance, and when we act in tune with them, we feel unfettered and motivated. It's very hard to motivate yourself if you are acting against your values — there's an inner conflict, a bit like trying to swim against the tide. It not only feels wrong, it's a real struggle.

Knowing your values will also explain why some situations make you feel so unsettled and anxious. For example, let's say you have a strong value around honesty. How are you going to feel if you are asked to behave unethically — whether it be to lie about a product or manipulate figures? It goes against the grain and is very uncomfortable to live with.

The truth is your life is unlikely to be fulfilling if you aren't living in line with your values, so that's why it's worth clarifying what they are!

EXERCISE: Your Values
1. Think of a time when you felt really passionate about something. Why did you feel that way? What was it that felt important to you?
2. What must you have in your life in order to be fulfilled?
3. What do people say about you? What do they tease you about, or complain about?
4. Think about times when you have been at your most absorbed in what you were doing. What was it? What made it feel so good?
5. Think about times when you have felt most upset, angry or frustrated. What was at the root of your feelings?

Now, have a go at making a list of your values. Choose

words or phrases that illustrate them, e.g. honesty, fun, security, fairness, loyalty, love, friendship, vitality, creativity, orderliness, harmony, intimacy, tradition, humour, freedom to choose, independence, adventure, beauty, excitement, being direct, justice, authenticity, good timekeeping..... you get the idea? This will help to clarify what really matters to you, and who you are when all the superficial 'stuff' is stripped away. Be quite spontaneous with this exercise — you can whittle it down afterwards.

How about taking that one stage further? If you were to think of one word (or phrase) that describes your 'brand' (or your 'essence'), what would it be? It can be anything at all. This exercise helps to refine the idea of who you are and reminds you of your own individuality and unique worth — which feels pretty empowering.

Imposter Syndrome

If you live with chronic self-doubt and worry about being exposed as a fraud, despite having been relatively successful, you may suffer from Imposter Syndrome. It's very common, with many of us feeling this way at some point in our lives, and it seems most common in women. It comes to the fore more when we have a change of environment, such as going to college or starting a new job. Whilst it also affects men, women seem to be held back by it to a greater extent.

Imposter Syndrome has found many followers amongst the members of the Good Girl club — women from around the world, from a wide range of backgrounds and from all religions, races and socio-economic classes. There are many successful, driven women who, despite plenty of evidence of their ability, secretly believe they don't deserve that success.

They discount the positive comments because they don't feel worthy of it. 'I'm just acting the role.... it's all smoke and mirrors.... I'm a fake.... I was just lucky.... it's just a matter of time before they realise.... it's only because I was in the right place at the right time.... they were being nice.' Recognise any of those thoughts?

The fear is usually about a lack of intelligence, ability or competence and whilst we mainly associate that with work, it can apply equally to other roles in life; anything from parenting to being on the running club committee.

How to combat Imposter Syndrome:
- Understand where it comes from and see it for the illusion that it is — one you have created, and which doesn't reflect reality. It's an out of date error message, which needs deleting.
- What story are you telling yourself that is maintaining and reinforcing that feeling? Confront some of those deeply held beliefs about yourself by writing down the negative thoughts which are keeping your Imposter Syndrome alive. Then beside each one come up with a more realistic and positive alternative. Add to the list regularly and really focus on replacing those thoughts as they come up. Create a new habit.
- Ask: does it make sense to see myself this way when others obviously see me differently?
- Don't compare yourself with other people. There will always be those who are more able and there will always be those who are less able than you. What's more, you don't know what that person has had to go through to be where they are. We each have our strengths and weaknesses, more or less

experience, and our own struggles. You don't have to be prefect or the best to be entitled to be where you are. And you don't have to be like anyone else, far from it; your value is in your individuality, your unique creative self. Don't be afraid to be you.

• You are entitled to make mistakes, just like everyone else. It's how we learn.

• Rationally assess your skills, experience and abilities. What have others said about you? What positive feedback came out of your performance review? I know how easy it is to focus on the few negative comments (we all have them)! Objectively consider where you are, what you are contributing and where you can improve. Be fair to yourself. See things in their true perspective, rather than through the lens of that inner critic.

• Make sure your body language reflects the new belief that you deserve to be where you are. For more on body language see Chapter 8.

Fear of success

Why might you be afraid of being successful? Well, if you're used to putting yourself under relentless pressure to be this or that, and you have a deeply held belief that you're not good enough, it's understandable you might hold back. You see, it's not fear of success, it's actually fear of failure. When the stakes appear high you might easily convince yourself that it would be a total disaster if you didn't instantly perform well. This can make Good Girls risk averse. They hide their light under a bushel and hesitate too long over going for a new opportunity.

There are other factors that might make us fearful about

putting ourselves out there. You might, for example, be concerned about upsetting other people. Would your partner support your desire for advancement? Is it possible you might not be so available to carry out the domestic responsibilities or to focus on their needs? Or perhaps a more senior role will mean stepping on a co-worker's toes or managing those you feel might resent it. If you were brought up with the 'don't show off' and 'who do you think you are' messages, you'll need to be brave and push through those if you are to get what you want.

You might even subconsciously sabotage your own efforts because it can be less scary to stay where you are than to venture into the uncharted waters of change. Does any of this ring true for you? Take a minute to think about it, and if there have been times when you avoided opportunities, recognise it and take the learning from it. There's no shame in acknowledging you were afraid. It's called being human.

However, now that you know a little more about your Good Girl and how she was created, you have greater self-awareness. This knowledge is a powerful thing. Is there a challenge or opportunity you could go after now, but have been too afraid to? What are three things you'll miss out on if you continue to play it safe? Perhaps now is the moment to choose change.

> *'Twenty years from now you will be more disappointed by the things you didn't do than by the things you did do. So throw off the bowlines. Sail away from the safe harbour. Catch the trade winds in your sails. Explore. Dream. Discover.'* MARK TWAIN

Strengthening your inner confidence

Take a moment to recall how you feel when your confidence is high. Do you feel light and buoyant, joyful, things flowing almost effortlessly? Perhaps it's because when we are truly expressing ourselves we are realising at least some of our potential as human beings. We are at our authentic best. We feel strong, powerful and fearless. Unfortunately, that feeling often seems to pass all too quickly, and that may be because it's usually associated with being good at a particular activity, as opposed to just being a valuable person.

Why does it seem so elusive sometimes and yet not at others? Why are we confident in some areas of our life and not in others? Even the seemingly most confident of us have periods when our self-confidence is low, or areas of our lives where we are more, or less confident. Perhaps you have no problem making a presentation to a roomful of people at work but get really anxious about having to ask your neighbour to turn the music down!

If we are to be truly confident, we need a healthy level of **self-esteem**. Self-esteem refers more to the overall opinion we have of ourselves and the basic value we put on ourselves as people. It is central to emotional well-being — without it we can't reach our full potential as human beings. It develops throughout our lives depending on our experiences; positive experiences enhance it, and negative experiences can undermine it.

We are all vulnerable in different ways, but if as a Good Girl your self-esteem is low, you will tend to view life through the filter of self-doubt and fear. And on the other hand, the higher your self-esteem the more likely that you'll see your problems and disappointments as solvable, rather than as negative experiences that go to the very root of your self-worth. When you have disappointments or failures in life, high self-esteem helps you to bounce back from them. To increase your self-esteem, start actively challenging those unhelpful beliefs, attitudes and thoughts!

It's about reminding yourself regularly that we're all different, each of us unique and special; there is no-one else like you in the whole world. That goes for each and every one of us. We have different values, different ways of seeing the world, different strengths... so what's the point in concentrating on your weaknesses? Instead focus on your strengths. Believe you are worth it, believe you deserve it, and believe you can have it. Why not you! Be yourself — be prepared to stand out!

VISUALISATION

Begin with the 'Relax and Focus Inwards' section as you did at the end of Chapter 5, i.e. finding a quiet place, using your breathing and some beautiful imagery to allow you to deepen your relaxation and drift into a feeling of comfort and well-being, then: continue with this session's visualisation.

Your Confidence is Growing

As you continue to focus inwards, imagine you are strolling in the countryside in springtime when you notice a pretty cottage set on the hillside, which seems deserted. As you get closer you can see it has the most glorious garden, full of many different flowers, shrubs and trees. But you notice that there is an area where only weeds are growing, and you decide you'll pull them up and tidy the area. So you set about the task of removing the weeds, some of which have quite deep roots.

123

Next, in order to finish the job, you sweep them all up and put them onto the compost heap at the back of the house.

As you stand back and admire your work, you put your hand in your pocket and pull out a small packet marked 'Magic Seeds', and of course, you decide to scatter them here. So after turning over the soil to make it ready, you sprinkle and water the seeds, feeling rather pleased with your efforts!

A month or so later you return to see how the garden is getting on and you're met with a riot of colour! So many flowers, beautiful colours swaying in the light breeze, insects buzzing busily, a heady perfume in the air. A newness, a freshness, yet warmed by the sunshine. Each seed has developed in its own unique way to reach its potential, each beautiful and knowing its worth, just like you. See yourself now, growing in your understanding of who you are, in touch with your true self, willing and able to show more of yourself and nurturing your own unique abilities.

Now gently bring yourself back to normal awareness, and back to your day, confident that you are releasing yourself from the influence of that Good Girl inside.

Chapter 8
Communicating Honestly and with Confidence

> *Remember this, you can't change anyone else's behaviour, only your own.*

I'd hazard a guess that you often find yourself agreeing to something you hadn't meant to, or realising you didn't say what you wanted to say. Many of us are brought up to be so afraid of confrontation that we'll do almost anything to avoid it, so we shy away from saying what we really think or feel and end up being railroaded. We want so much to be liked and not to cause trouble that we forget we have a responsibility to ourselves. Then there's a good chance that others will take advantage. Perhaps not intentionally — but nevertheless they will.

Bear in mind that much of our behaviour is automatic — the unconscious mind is running the show most of the time. We might think we're choosing how to react, but when it comes to our relationships with others, in the main we simply repeat old patterns and involve ourselves in the same old games. You know the ones I mean. Games of 'he says this, so I say that', or 'I do this, so she does that'. We don't even know we're doing it most of the time. Have a think and see if you can identify the games you play, in the different areas of your life. Don't think about who's to blame, just be objective. Start by simply identifying some typical conversations between you and someone with whom you have a difficult relationship, where perhaps you often end up feeling angry or upset. Do you experience these interactions most often at home, at work or socially?

Remember this: you can't change anyone else's behaviour, only your own. But because all interactions are dynamic, when you behave differently, even if it feels unnatural for you, the amazing thing is the other person generally responds differently too. Confidence is key, and the great thing is that you don't have to actually believe you are a confident person, you can learn to act 'as if' — faking it until you feel it. More about how to do that in a moment. Slowly, as you repeat these changes, acting in a more self-assured way more of the time, you will see the benefits and notice how much better you feel.

As you start to internalise that confidence, making it real, you go from feeling taken for granted to having a more positive, more balanced understanding of your options. You will hopefully begin to see the way forward and feel more in control of your life. You don't have to do it perfectly. Be patient with yourself; it may take time, but every time you get a positive result or notice an improvement, however small, make sure you make a mental note of it. You might even write it down in your journal so you can refer back to it and help boost your confidence at a later date.

So let's get down to the detail.

Knowing what you want

As a Good Girl you may be so used to anticipating the expectations of others that you don't really have a clear idea of what you actually want. Perhaps you know what you <u>don't</u> want, but that's not the same thing. How can you communicate your thoughts, opinions and needs to other people if you aren't clear about the outcome you want? What are you okay with, what are your boundaries, and how far are you prepared to negotiate? Consider again those difficult conversations that seem to happen all too often. How do they normally play out and how do you feel afterwards? What would you like to have happened? What would be a better outcome? Only when you can answer those questions can you work out your strategy for achieving that.

Without this kind of clarity, we can't be true to ourselves, and this can lead to depression, anxiety, feelings of resentment, anger and guilt. To really blossom as yourself, to have healthy, honest relationships and make the most of your unique talents, it's important to become comfortable with being more assertive.

Knowing your Rights

We hear that word 'assertive' bandied about quite often, but what does it really mean? Well, it's definitely not about being overbearing or loud, or getting what you want all the time. It's a way of feeling in control and not allowing emotions to overwhelm you. It allows you to express powerful feelings like anger or frustration appropriately. It's about demonstrating active listening skills; then there is more chance you too will be listened to with greater respect.

It means standing up for your own rights, but at the same

time respecting the rights of others. It's about direct, honest communication, and about taking responsibility for your own communication and behaviour. It's not about being passive — which is putting up with all sorts, and it's also very much not being aggressive — which is getting your own way no matter what. If you normally err on the side of being non-assertive, then someone who is acting assertively might appear aggressive to you. But that's because you are looking at it from your own unique perspective! To you they seem too pushy because their behaviour would be so unnatural for you.

First of all, let's look at your basic human rights. There are a few versions of this list, but generally speaking they include the following:

Basic Human Rights

- The right to state my own needs and set my own priorities, regardless of any roles or responsibilities that I have taken on in my life.
- The right to be treated with respect as an equal human being, regardless of my colour, race, creed or gender.
- The right to express my feelings and emotions in an appropriate way.
- The right to express my opinions and values and to have them respected.
- The right to say 'yes' or 'no' for myself.
- The right to make mistakes.
- The right to change my mind.
- The right to say, 'I do not understand' and ask for more information.
- The right to ask for something I want (whilst acknowledging the other person's right to say 'No'!).
- The right to deal with situations and other people as I feel appropriate, without feeling dependent on others for

approval.
- The right to choose not to get involved in other people's problems.

Does anything on that list surprise you? You may not have ever thought about it in these terms before, but it does make good common sense and is worth taking a moment to consider in terms of your own life. One client told me, 'I have always felt that if I am able to do something to help someone, then I also have a duty to do so. It has tripped me up more than once, as I have found that sometimes people want empathy, not solutions.' That duty word again. What is the price you've paid for not standing up for yourself, for instance? You have more freedom than you think and are entitled to expect more consideration than you realise.

It's not easy to get right, this assertiveness business. I still struggle. I wish it were otherwise, but my embedded Good Girl is still over-sensitive to what others might think. When I'm feeling particularly vulnerable, I will probably always have a tendency to take things personally, feel defensive, and assume people are upset or annoyed with me. That's just how it is. However, the difference is that now I'm much more likely to run it past my internal editor and therefore much less likely to allow it to be reflected in my behaviour. I've learnt that if I can stay in control of how I respond, the outcome is usually more positive.

Becoming More Assertive

As you read the following four main behaviours you might identify more with one style than the others, but it's important to be clear that YOU ARE NOT YOUR

BEHAVIOUR. Whilst you may tend to use one style more often, you will also behave differently at other times or in other situations. Remember that at any moment you can consciously **choose** to behave differently, and in that moment you can potentially change the outcome of any interaction. That's how you create new habits.

THE 4 BEHAVIOURS
Understanding assertiveness is easier if we see it as one of the four behaviours we have to choose from at any given time:

<u>Aggressive Behaviour</u>: The main features are: **dominating, bullying, loud, impatient, angry, rigid, intolerant, in your personal space, staring, pointing, intimidating, or violent**. It's 'I WIN' behaviour. I think we all know how aggression presents itself. There are many reasons why we might act this way and they are very much about us and not the other person. When we feel unable to express our feelings honestly and our anger constructively, when we feel unable to ask for what we need, this can lead to high levels of frustration. If we feel criticised, we might react defensively and end up being aggressive, which hardly ever advances our cause.

<u>Passive Aggressive Behaviour</u>: The main features are: **sulking, manipulating, sarcasm, being withdrawn, blaming, goading, withholding information, sabotaging, gossiping, emotional blackmail.** Once again, this is also 'I WIN' behaviour. Most Good Girls are quite shocked when they realise how often they use a passive aggressive style in their conversations. It is sometimes called 'indirect or covert aggression', because, although it presents itself in different

clothes, it is still a form of aggression. The aim is still to gain advantage (as with aggression) but instead by using subterfuge or manipulation, basically doing whatever it takes to avoid confrontation. Imagine this scenario: your partner is preoccupied and you feel he's ignoring you. Do you deal with it in a mature, open and honest way? It will depend on your mood but probably not. Instead you might sulk or make a sarcastic remark such as 'you've always got time for everyone else but me!' Am I right?

This is actually quite childlike behaviour. Imagine another scenario, this time at work. Jane is upset because the promotion she so badly wanted has been given to someone from outside the company. When the new person, Heather, arrives to start in the role she's aware that Jane is rather unforthcoming and off-hand but she can't understand why. Rather than helping her get to grips with things, Jane deliberately withholds information and watches while she falls foul of office politics, secretly happy to see Heather struggle. Not especially attractive behaviour and not something we would want to be true of ourselves, but if you're being honest, you might recall having acted this way.

And when you're on the receiving end of passive aggressive behaviour it can make you feel really guilty. Imagine this. You go to visit your elderly mother in residential care. You are living and working some way away but usually manage to get to see her every week. On one occasion you explain that it would probably be two weeks before your next visit because of being away with work. You love your mum very much but she isn't above a little emotional blackmail. 'Don't worry about me, Ros, I'll be all right,' she says. In themselves those words sound fine, but add in the 'poor me' intonation and it triggers that familiar guilty feeling in you.

Passive Behaviour The main features are: **intimidated, can't say no, like a 'door mat', don't speak up, no eye contact, defensive body language, agree when you don't really, submissive, putting up with all sorts for an easy life.** In other words, 'YOU WIN'. If you're someone who will do anything to avoid conflict, then behaving this way will be familiar to you, to a greater or lesser extent. It can be painful to admit that you've given in way too often — sometimes just for a quiet life, sometimes because it doesn't matter all that much, sometimes because you don't have the energy or don't know what you want to say. You may not want to rock the boat or risk being wrong.

At other times you may have missed out on what you wanted to do or not had your opinion heard. That can make you feel stupid and then angry and resentful. But to be fair, if you haven't spoken up, you can't really expect your views to be heard and your needs to be met!

Assertive behaviour: The main features are: **confident, open, honest, tolerant, respectful of others, sensitive, co-operative, grounded, objective, willing to listen, clear, direct.** Ideally we both win, so 'WIN/ WIN'. Being assertive is what we need to aim for, because it means standing up for ourselves whilst being sensitive to and respecting the rights of others. It's about direct, honest communication, and taking responsibility for what you say (and how you say it) and what you do. You look for ways of co-operating or compromising, and you take your time to respond, rather than allowing the knee-jerk reaction associated with a lack of control.

It's often more difficult to be assertive with those closest to us because it's so easy to be derailed by our emotions. But as you learn the skills involved you find your self-confidence and self-esteem enhanced in all areas of life. A word of caution: your family, friends, colleagues may be caught off guard by your newfound willingness to be assertive. Be prepared for a period of adjustment. It takes time, so don't be put off by the occasional difficulty. There will always be occasions when you find it more difficult, when you don't feel well or your energy is low, for instance. Be kind to yourself, take it slowly at first and practise on the less important issues, then as you gradually gain confidence, you'll become more skilled in this new way of communicating. You'll also learn to listen to your intuition as you become more experienced. That means you will have a better feel for when to push for something and when to let it go. Keep at it and the pay-off will be worth all the effort, I promise.

The Secrets of Assertiveness
• **Boost your confidence beforehand if you can.** A confident frame of mind is the foundation and makes all the difference to how well you get your opinions heard. Think about what you want, obstacles you might face and how to overcome them. Get yourself into a positive, focused frame of mind and recall a time when you felt really good about yourself, full of confidence and on top of things. It can be anything at all, it doesn't have to be a world-shattering achievement. Or bringing to mind a personal role model can help. Is there a friend or colleague, or even a character from TV or a film you admire and whom you would like to emulate?

In the jobs I've had, I have found it really helpful to observe those who were more experienced than me — in particular listening to how they handle problem phone calls. There's no substitute for experience but, for example, where an important customer is considering cancelling an order, if you <u>can</u> short-cut the need to reinvent the wheel every time, then why not?

Think of someone who seems to have a natural confidence, who communicates easily and positively. Imagine you could take on their qualities, perhaps put on their jacket and channel their confidence. Try it now and see how it changes the way you feel. It's a great technique because it's quick to get your head around and engages both mind and body instantly.

• **Be clear and direct, open and honest.** I can recall times where I talked nervously for far too long, trying to explain myself, and not helping matters at all. Picture this: you've decided to ask your boss for a pay rise and you've finally summoned up the courage to approach the subject. You haven't really prepared what to say and you're feeling understandably nervous. You launch in, covering all the reasons why you feel overlooked, why it's deserved, talking too fast and for too long. Your tone might be needy, and instead of just focusing on your own achievements in order to justify the increase, you complain about what some of your colleagues are being paid, for doing less work. And you forget to actually ask for what you want! Of course, you might need to be flexible, but if you don't know what you're aiming for, you probably won't get it.

• **So know what you want**, rehearse it and say it concisely. Use short sentences. Repeat if necessary. Focus your mind. Stick to the subject, don't get side-tracked and keep the end in mind. Check again — what is the outcome you want?

• **Watch your internal chatter.** What is the story you are telling yourself about this situation? Be positive and say something helpful to yourself, such as 'I can handle this' or 'It's okay'. What images are you running through your mind when you anticipate having to put your point across? Are you seeing the other person with an angry or unkind face? Are they behaving negatively towards you? Now replace that negative image with a positive one. Imagine yourself relaxed, communicating with ease and see the other person smiling amenably. See things working out well.

• **Active listening.** This is a key communication skill and one we use far too little. People just don't listen to each other. We make big assumptions about what others will say, without actually listening, and we are at our worst with those who are close to us. When someone feels heard they visibly relax and become more reasonable. This is the Chinese character for the word 'to listen'. We have to <u>give</u> what it is we want, in order to receive it back, and what a gift we give to someone when we really listen to them, when we give them our time and undivided attention. In a social situation, for example, if you want to engage with someone, you don't necessarily have to be especially interesting. If you show a genuine interest in them, they tend to see you as interesting! And that makes it easier to relax and say what you want to say. Whatever the situation, remember that actively listening does NOT show weakness — it's the opposite. What's more, it pays dividends.

聽

ear → 聽 ← you
← eyes
← undivided attention
← heart

'Courage is what it takes to stand up and speak; courage is also what it takes to sit down and listen.'
SIR WINSTON CHURCHILL

- **Use 'I' statements**. If you want to be heard, it's important to take responsibility for your own feelings and for the way you give voice to them. No-one can actually argue that your feelings are not valid when you express them as your own, for example 'I feel annoyed when…' as opposed to 'You make me angry when…'

- **Watch your language carefully.** When you feel anxious or angry you are more likely to exaggerate, take things personally, and become defensive. Do you sometimes hear yourself as you fan the flames with overly emotional language? Make a real effort to remain calm, looking for solutions and compromise, and eventually it will come more easily.

- **Criticise the behaviour** and <u>not</u> the person. Remember we are <u>not</u> our behaviour; it is something which we choose, consciously or unconsciously, but it's not who we are. People can change. You might be tempted to follow an automatic pattern and say something which would make it about the whole person like, 'You're just mean and couldn't care less about me'. Better to try, 'I feel hurt when you behave in that controlling way' or 'I'd prefer it if you asked me first before making decisions that affect me'. Remember that it's important to ask for the change you want instead of just complaining, blaming or 'whinging'. That's passive aggressive and actually makes you feel more stressed — because you have now cast yourself in the role of victim.

• **Choose Your Battles.** Having decided you want to be more assertive, don't go at it full tilt. Decide which battles to fight, remain flexible but know your limits — when to press forward and when to let go. There's no need to change your personality. You are still you, but now you're letting people see more of who you are.

• **How to say 'No'.** When you choose to say 'Yes' to yourself, that means sometimes saying 'No' to the requests of others. By valuing yourself and your time, you recognise your right to make your own priorities. Firstly, you need to have decided you do indeed want to say 'No', and then make a commitment to do just that. But you will need to be prepared, as your impulse will be to say 'Yes', because it's easier and pleases others. They will seek to catch you off guard, speaking to your emotions, perhaps appealing to your better nature and arousing feelings of sympathy or obligation. They might get angry or attempt to blind you with their clever, persuasive argument. Your Good Girl will also try to derail your attempts to say the dreaded 'No' word. She'll do anything to avoid discomfort, conflict or guilt, so will be trying to creep through the cracks in your resolve.

Be ready with some helpful thoughts or positive affirmations, such as 'I'll stick to my plan', 'I'll feel stressed if I agree', 'I have a duty to myself', 'Even if I feel sorry for her, I'll be firm'. You can only convince others if you yourself are convinced.

It's really useful to have some idea of your tactics when in this kind of situation. Think about the next time you might be wanting to say 'No' and consider these questions:

-I want to say 'No' because...

-They are likely to try to persuade me by...

-The emotions they are trying to arouse in me are...

-I want to remind myself with these positive affirmations...

-When faced with their persuasive tactics I will say...

-The benefits of having said 'No' are...

Next visualise yourself in the situation with the person involved and see it going well. To give yourself a better chance of success, regularly practise the visualisation at the end of this chapter.

Just a few thoughts on how we say 'No'. You may have attended an assertiveness training course and found yourself thinking that there's no way you could just say 'No, I can't do that' or 'Well, I want this'. We live in a society, certainly here in the UK, which values courtesy, and so in my view we're most likely to succeed when we work with that. It's a personal opinion but if I need to say 'No', I'm happy to soften the edges by saying, 'Sorry I can't do that for you — I'm too busy at the moment' or '...it makes me feel uncomfortable', or 'it's not my thing'. Saying sorry in this context is fine, it's not the same as being unnecessarily apologetic, which is very different.

The way we say the word 'No' is almost more important than the word itself. Try this — ideally when no-one else is around! Look in the mirror and say 'No' in as many different ways as you can. You'll make yourself laugh if nothing else. Sometimes we're so worried that the other person will try to persuade us that we blurt it out, sounding more aggressive than we had intended. Then we feel guilty and don't quite know how to revisit it. Relax — there is no need to rush. Take your time to say it clearly, but in a way you feel happy with. And you'll soon learn that, amazing as it might sound, **nothing dreadful happens when you say 'No'.**

> '*One key to successful relationships is learning to say no without guilt, so that you can say yes without resentment.*'
> BILL CRAWFORD

• **Sell the benefits.** If you want to sway someone over to your point of view, whether at work or at home, why not suggest an incentive that will encourage co-operation? For example, 'If I'm given overall responsibility for the project, it's going to be much easier to make decisions on the ground, rather than bothering you with every detail' or 'If you help me now, we can get out sooner.'

• **Asking for help** if you need it. I don't mean in a helpless 'I can't manage it on my own' puppy dog way. If you're at work and need something explaining to you or you need more resources in order to do your job effectively, it's incumbent upon you to ask for help. Or perhaps you want more help with the household chores, or need the support of a friend. If you need help, then take a breath and ask. That's the right thing to do. It's actually empowering because showing honesty and vulnerability is a strength — it helps us connect with each other and in a more meaningful way. What's more, if you don't ask, you don't get. How will anyone know if you don't say something? You're a human being, not superwoman, so you might as well come to terms with the idea. And anyway, martyrdom is <u>so</u> overrated.

• **Take your time** and use calm, deep breaths if you are feeling anxious. You might feel rushed when someone is pressurising you, but why allow them to set the pace? Say so if you need to give it some thought and defer the conversation to a later time. If it's just a question of giving yourself a moment to regroup, then make an excuse to leave the room so you can return feeling slightly more grounded.

• **Time and Place.** Being assertive in a spontaneous way has both advantages and disadvantages. It means that the feelings are dealt with there and then — they don't have time to build up causing long-lasting ill feeling or an explosion later on. Not being assertive at the time also means there's a risk that the issue will never be resolved because it's difficult to go back to sort it out at a later date. On the other hand, it may not always be the best idea to act spontaneously. Feelings may be running high — then a cooling-off time is the solution. It may also not be appropriate; if it's in public, for example, or the other person is too preoccupied to listen. This would make it difficult to have an open, honest, assertive exchange. I'm not advocating you walk on eggshells, but there may be a time and place where you stand a better chance of being heard.

• **Finally - stop being so damned nice**! It's such hard work being nice all the time. It drains away your self-respect and it won't get you what you want. Stop apologising when you don't mean it. Stop worrying about what people think and concentrate on getting what you want by being a grounded, fair and reasonable adult.

Your Body Language

This is a fascinating subject and much has been written about it over the last 20 years. For most of us, though, body language is still a little understood aspect of our interactions with others. We <u>do</u> on one level understand more than we think and we respond to it intuitively, but most of it is so extraordinarily subtle and sub-conscious that we don't always pick up on it.

Whether or not we realise it we are continually sending out and receiving non-verbal signals through body posture, gestures, facial expressions, tone of voice and so on. These signals are reflections of our true feelings and emotions. When we are disapproving, even if our words are not critical, it may come across in more subtle ways, such as arm folding, frowning, eye rolling, accusing tone and so on. Those people with well-developed emotional antennae will be more instinctively able than others to pick up such signals, but we can all learn to read them, allowing us to 'hear' more of the truth in the message. But it's important to look at the whole person rather than focus on one aspect of body language — for example, when we cross our arms it's not always defensive. Sometimes it's because we're cold!

We can also use this knowledge to adjust our own body language in order to appear more positive, confident and assertive.

<u>Submissive Body Language</u>

It's not always that obvious that someone has a secret Good Girl inside. For me, as with most Good Girls, she comes to the fore in particular situations.

Most of my young years were spent feeling like an outsider, because of the different places we lived in and the constant change of school. So I was acutely aware of any way in which I was different. A couple of examples come to mind that illustrate how my body language manifested that inner Good Girl.

Making yourself 'small' because you don't deserve to take up too much space is classic. Picture this, age 11 in the senior school morning assembly, I'm standing in the front row. I'm acutely and painfully aware that I'm quite a lot taller than the other girls (it probably seemed more obvious than it actually was), so I try to make myself less obvious by shrinking and subtly bending my knees! As I grew older there weren't many boys my age who were taller than me, and on the rare occasion that I dated someone shorter than me I felt ridiculously self-conscious — I'd do anything to appear shorter! How I feel for that younger me. I wish I could have told her what I know now. I would have said, 'Stop discounting yourself and sitting on the bottom shelf — elevate yourself to the premium brand shelf where you belong. Stand tall.'

Another time I recall I was much older, working for an international publisher and regularly travelling by air for my work. I was seated in between two men. Perfectly pleasant guys, I'm sure, and I've no reason to think this was personal, but I suddenly noticed that, whereas my hands were in my lap, they took up all the arm rests without a second thought. And whereas I sat with my knees together they had theirs splayed out, looking relaxed and comfortable.

Is there an argument that men feel more comfortable that way because of their physical difference? I can't say one way or the other and that discussion would open up a whole separate can of worms. Anyway, from that moment I decided I was entitled to the same as them. I relaxed more into my allotted space and took possession of at least one arm. I never looked back after that.

I would like to think that this kind of modesty is less common now, but everywhere we can see women teetering on ridiculously high heels, dressing to please men and at the same time making themselves small. One thing that drives me crazy is that helpless coquettish look some women use — head tilted down and to one side, eyes looking upwards but not making eye contact. 'I'm no threat, I'm just a poor down-trodden little girl,' they say. Hair twiddling and flicking, fidgeting and hand wringing show self-consciousness and a degree of anxiety.

How you sound is a key aspect of how you come across. If you want to be taken seriously, at work in particular, it will be more difficult if you are quietly spoken, especially so if you use a timid, little girl tone. Much of this is learnt behaviour and behind the mask of subservience is often a much stronger, sharper and more opinionated woman. It's the fear of being wrong or upsetting someone that makes her stay quiet. Even if asked she might appear unsure of herself, saying, 'Would it be all right with you if...', or 'I'm not really sure, I could be wrong, of course...', and apologising a lot. Next time you're in a group or a formal meeting and you see a colleague sitting with her hand or finger over her mouth, it shows she's probably trying hard to stop herself from speaking up.

Confident Body Language
• Take up your space. Keep your body open and relaxed with natural gestures. Sit or stand more upright, literally 'stand

up for yourself'. If you lean forward a little rather than being too 'laid back', you will appear more engaged in the conversation. Easy, open gestures show emphasis without aggression.

• <u>Good eye contact,</u> not holding the person's gaze in an uncomfortable (or even weird) way but if you are communicating sincerely, it should come relatively naturally. This communicates directness and a powerful message that you mean what you say. Just a point to remember here — cultural norms vary around the world when it comes to this, and in many cultures direct eye contact might be seen as rude or aggressive.

• <u>Facial expression</u>. This should match what you are saying and be genuine. If you say 'No', it's not going to give that message if you're smiling. It says 'I can probably be persuaded'.

• <u>Your voice</u> should be clear and strong, your tone well-modulated. Be careful not to use a high-pitched whining or pleading tone. Apparently, children often give more attention and respect to their father's voice because it sounds firmer and more serious. Mothers often use a rather pleading style with their children which the kids find easier to ignore. I guess it's also partly because the kids become more immune to the sound of Mum's voice if she's the main caregiver. To become more aware of the volume of your voice, practise alternating between speaking loudly and then softly. You can also play with the pitch and tone to see how that feels.

• <u>When discussing a problem between you,</u> instead of standing or sitting directly opposite the other person, which can feel adversarial, try placing yourself **diagonally** to them and imagining the problem 'over there'. It's a more collaborative approach and really works well.

• <u>Email or Text.</u> There are major pitfalls associated with electronic conversations as most of us know from bitter experience. Not being able to see or hear them makes it very easy to misinterpret what people write. I've had a few clients who suggested I trawl through long text conversations on their phone to help work out what their boyfriend or girlfriend is really saying! I decline the offer and suggest they either meet up or speak on the phone.

The key thing to remember with texting especially, is that it's even <u>more</u> important not to jump to hasty conclusions about the meaning. If it's ambiguous, seek clarification. If you're a sensitive Good Girl, you may find that some people are too direct, sounding almost rude when they email. Be aware of their style and take account of it. Don't make meaning where there is none.

Similarly, whilst you will want to appear polite and courteous, be careful not to go all round the houses, littering your emails with too much submissive 'soft' language, like 'I wonder if you'd mind…if it would be all right with you…if it's no trouble'. You get the idea.

<u>Matching, Pacing and Leading</u>. Building rapport is essential if you want to influence another person. It creates an atmosphere of trust, understanding and respect. When people are getting along, they naturally begin to co-ordinate their movements — this is known as 'Mirroring', like creating a mirror image. If one person's head is slightly cocked to the side, or legs crossed a certain way, you may notice the other's is too. So it can be a useful tip to remember — when you match a person's posture, tone or pace you are more able to build rapport and gain their

co-operation. By the way, you can match someone's pace and energy without also reflecting their heightened emotion. When you match in this way you can then 'pace and lead' — in other words lead them to behave in a calmer and more considered way.

For a really in-depth look at how to really listen and express yourself more effectively, I recommend an excellent book called *Nonviolent Communication: A Language of life* by Marshall B. Rosenberg. It's not about violence in the normal sense of the word, rather about communicating in a non-confrontational way.

VISUALISATION

<u>Begin</u> with the 'Relax and Focus Inwards' section as you did at the end of Chapter 5, i.e. finding a quiet place, using your breathing and some beautiful imagery to allow you to deepen your relaxation as you drift into a feeling of comfort and well-being, then continue with this session's visualisation:

Your Assertive Self

So now think of a person with whom you'd like to be more assertive; where you want to stand firm, say what needs to be said to make your point and stay calm at the same time.

Next, think of a particular situation with this person that is likely to crop up, and let's work with that. You're going to see yourself thinking, feeling and behaving differently. Imagine preparing yourself by getting into a confident frame of mind beforehand. Use lots of positive self-talk, reminding yourself you're okay, you're strong, that you can do this and seeing it turning out well. You look and feel grounded and confident. Now you're face-to-face, your voice clear and strong, firm but friendly. You take your time, you listen and remain steady and calm. You express yourself easily, breathing away any anxiety easily. You see things clearly and in their true perspective.

Imagine the other person looking engaged, responding more positively and showing more respect. Perhaps you can sense they are beginning to see you in a new light.

Perhaps you can imagine a character from a cartoon, film or book that represents confidence and strength? Or is there someone you know that you admire for their ability to remain calm and assertive when needed? Now take on their characteristics, stepping into their shoes. You're feeling more self-assured, rising above any doubts, feeling grounded and centred... and seeing the positive outcome you desire.

Now gently bring yourself back to normal awareness, and back to your day, confident that you are releasing yourself from the influence of that Good Girl inside.

Chapter 9
Engaging Your Adult Self

> '*For in every adult there dwells the child that was, and in every child there lies the adult that will be.*'
> **JOHN CONNOLLY**

If you want to be heard, if you want to get your point across effectively, the key is to keep your emotions under control. The more important the conversation, the more you worry about your feelings getting the better of you. Let's look at some ideas to help you stay in control.

Managing your emotions under pressure

It's important to get your anxious, angry or hurt feelings under control before a difficult conversation, so give yourself some positive self-talk, relax, do some breathing exercises and remind yourself you can do this.

Try not to anticipate difficulty because that can become a self-fulfilling prophecy. In other words, you're so convinced it will all go badly that your behaviour contributes to that very outcome. Expect things to go well, visualise it going well, but if you're concerned, why not talk it over with someone beforehand? Getting the problem out in the open where you can see it helps gives it structure and allows you to see it in perspective. Then you can work out your options for approaching the discussion. Using calm deep breaths, relaxing your body, staying centred and maintaining open body language will all help. Remember you have a responsibility to yourself to speak up, and you have the right to do that.

During the conversation notice those personal warning signs that tell you you're getting upset or angry. Either act to reduce the emotion or take a break until another time. If things get very heated, your brain will be 'flooded' with stress hormones and since it can take up to 20 minutes for normal levels to return, again taking time out may well be the best course of action.

Also be aware that when feelings run high there's a tendency to exaggerate, and if you do that, then the other person is likely to become defensive and find it difficult to engage honestly.

A real hot button for many of us is when we feel criticised. When this happens, do you shrink, feel small and become passive, or go straight into defensive mode? Instead of allowing that knee-jerk reaction, first stop, breathe and do nothing. Take a moment to consider what's <u>actually</u> being said, because it's easy to get it wrong when you have a rush of emotion. Try to remain in your objective, adult state, maybe asking for more information or clarification, be honest and open. Take your time, and remember to **respond rather than react.** If it is fair criticism, you may not like it but accept it, or part of it. If you disagree, then say so clearly and confidently — it's actually quite liberating. And if you prefer to have time to think, then say so.

As a Good Girl you know you have a tendency to worry too much about what others think of you. Okay, this is important — you don't need to feel responsible for the other person's reaction. Whatever the situation whether at home, at work or with your friends, if you're being fair, respectful and reasonable and have expressed your needs sensitively and respectfully, then their response is about <u>them</u>. It belongs to them and is not to do with you. It's not your fault.

Try not to ruminate over an uncomfortable exchange. As I've said before, Good Girls have this tendency to continually replay or mentally rehearse difficult encounters. You beat yourself up about what you did or said 'wrong' and torture yourself by reliving and magnifying embarrassing moments. Instead take any learning from it, and then be firm with yourself. <u>Stop</u>. Does it really matter? Tell yourself to lighten up, not to take yourself so damned seriously! It might seem important now, but given a day or so it will have faded into history. Why suffer when you don't need to?

Parent, Adult or Child?
Think of a time when someone was critical towards you — perhaps aggressive or belittling. How did you feel? Did you feel somewhat childlike and even react that way?

Wouldn't it be great if you could break the pattern and respond more objectively? Try as we may we can't change other people but when we change our <u>own</u> behaviour, we set in motion a whole new dynamic — and our difficult conversations suddenly have a more positive outcome. We know that new habits take time to establish and you will certainly fall back into your old ways now and again, but the results will speak for themselves and that will motivate you to keep at it.

The **Parent Adult Child** model, from the Transactional

Analysis theory of personality and personal change, is a tool used by many therapists. But its brilliant simplicity means it can be used effectively at many different levels — for therapists to explore in depth, but equally to help with everyday relationship or communication problems, at work or at home. It's an especially helpful tool for the Good Girl, as you will see.

It goes like this: within each of us are three 'ego' states — the Parent, the Adult and the Child — and we can choose to operate from any one of those, at any given moment.

The Parent is our inner voice of authority (can be Controlling and Critical OR it can be Nurturing), like a recording from our actual parents, teachers or other authority figures. It is made up of a huge number of hidden and overt 'messages', sometimes half-heard or half-understood but accepted as the truth by our younger self. It is **our 'taught' self**.

The Child is all about our internal reactions and feelings as we try to make sense of the world in our young years (up to about age 6). We can be in our Adaptive Child which often struggles to make sense of the world and can be resistant OR in our more spontaneous, Free Child. It's basically the emotional data within each of us. When we feel angry, upset, fearful or depressed, the Child is in control. When we are playful or freely expressing joy, the Child is also in control. Because of childhood experiences some find it difficult to be playful as adults, to express their Free Child. The Child is **the 'feeling' self**.

The Adult is where we think objectively and determine action for ourselves, based on our experience, and it is the way in which we keep our Parent and Child under control. If we are to change our Parent or Child state, this must usually be done through our Adult, **our 'thinking' self.**

When two people are communicating it is normally best if both are operating from the same ego state. So if both are in Critical Parent mode, for instance, complaining about the bus being late, that's fine. Or if in Free Child mode e.g. playing or making love, that's fine too.

The main problem comes when there is a 'crossed' transaction — the most common of which is when one person is communicating from their Critical Parent state the other person will often find themselves reacting from their Child state. And when the Child comes forward you are unlikely to be assertive or rational.

Generally speaking, then, it is best if we are able to communicate from our Adult state; it's the most effective means of achieving healthy communication. So what can you do to get out of the game? As I've said before, we can't change other people. However, we can influence the situation and prevent it from getting out of hand. Here's the key — if you want to move the other person into their reasonable Adult state, <u>you have to get into <i>your</i> Adult state</u>. When you do that, there's a good chance you will pull them into theirs. Here's an example of a situation where previously you might have reacted badly to your demanding, critical boss:

Boss (in his Critical Parent): 'I told you to get that report to me by today, so where is it? If I don't have those figures for the board meeting tomorrow, it'll be down to you.'

You (in your Adult): 'I'm so sorry I haven't been able to finish it. As you know, Mike has been away and I've had his

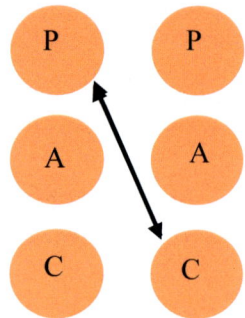

clients on the phone all day. I know it's not ideal, but I'm working on it now, and I'll get it to you first thing tomorrow in plenty of time for your meeting.'

At this point, even though he might not be happy, your boss is now less likely to continue with his aggressive tone. You are being assertive and reasonable, taking a problem-solving approach to the issue. Sometimes it takes a few attempts, but it works most of the time. You are no longer playing the game, and since that takes two, neither is he! Knowing about this theory could help you in many situations.

Emotions tend to be less under control in our personal relationships, so these roles can sometimes swap around quite quickly. Suddenly the person in the Critical Parent state might try another ploy and swap into their 'poor me' Child state, and that shifts you into Critical Parent role — and the 'game' continues.

A question for you — how often do *you* operate in your Critical Parent or Child state? Does this model remind you of any recurring patterns with your partner or other family members?

So, each of us can, at any given time, be in either our Parent, Adult or Child state. When you find yourself listening to that negative critical voice in your head, you are in your Critical Parent mode. The same applies when you're being very hard on yourself, beating yourself up over something you've done or said. Similarly, when that 'poor me' voice is in charge you are also not in your Adult place, but in your Child instead. Get into the habit of noticing when this is happening and make an active shift into your Adult self. Perhaps put your Adult hat on, whatever metaphor works for you. Imagine what your Adult self would be saying to you, and notice how different you feel. It gets easier each time you make this shift, so practise regularly.

Victim No More

Whether we are aware of it or not, many of us will spend much of our time reacting to life as victims. Whenever we avoid taking responsibility for ourselves, we are unconsciously choosing to react in this way. Good Girls in particular often fall into the trap of being too understanding, too tolerant, too helpful and too modest. All of these are forms of female submission and in choosing to behave this way we cast ourselves as victims. It's no wonder then that we might feel unfulfilled at best, resentful and depressed at worst.

The Drama Triangle is a simple yet powerful model for interpreting these victim-based 'games'. It was devised in 1968 by psychiatrist Dr Stephen Karpman, a teacher of Transactional Analysis, and has helped countless people to understand the dynamics of their dysfunctional interactions. It dovetails nicely with the Parent Adult Child model above.

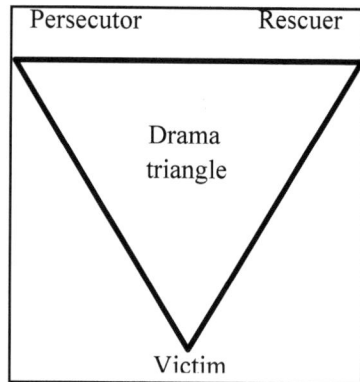

Persecutor · Rescuer · Drama triangle · Victim

It's a valuable therapeutic tool, particularly when working with addiction and relationship issues, but it could help you too. The triangle is made up of three different roles, Victim, Rescuer and Persecutor, but essentially, they are all about victimhood and its various faces, and come from feelings of shame or worthlessness. We tend to have our preferred role, and each role has its own starting position, which is the one we adopted as a young child:

The Victim: The door-mat. Feels persecuted, unappreciated, helpless. This starting position is 'I'm the problem', 'There's something wrong with me', 'Poor me'. Perhaps you were called naughty or selfish, or for some reason were over-protected. No surprise that you need a Rescuer to fix you, or you look for a Persecutor to belittle you, because both will reinforce that negative view of yourself, the one that feels familiar. You tend to feel overwhelmed by your vulnerability. You feel slighted or wronged. You blame others when things go wrong. You may find yourself often saying 'yes, but...'

The Rescuer: The do-gooder. 'I'll look after you'. This starting position is 'I must help others in order to be loved'. You need someone to rescue in order to feel important and valued. You may feel over-burdened, over-responsible, perhaps a bit of a martyr. It seems that you're the one who has to sort everything out! You can see how easy it is to become resentful.

The Persecutor: The bully. Controls, blames or criticises in order to feel powerful. Contrary to how it might appear, this starting position is defensive, 'the world is a dangerous place so I have to get them before they get me!' Do you put others down and feel everything has to be done your way?

Here's how the triangle might look in action. *Let me introduce you to Jim (in his Victim state), who has an issue with Dave (in his Persecutor state). At lunch one day Jim*

155

confides in his colleague Sally (in her Rescuer state). He tells her all about his problems with Dave, saying he feels bullied and undermined by him. Sally decides she needs to do something to help the situation, and so she talks to Dave about the problem. Jim didn't expect her to do this! He now feels really anxious about the repercussions and is angry with Sally for getting involved. So there's been a swap around. Now Jim has moved into 'Persecutor' role and Sally is in 'Victim' mode, thinking Jim is ungrateful. It's so unfair; she was only trying to help!

Here's another one. *Imagine this — it's Christmas time and everyone is leaving all the preparations to you. You're feeling put upon and very much in your 'poor me', 'I can't cope' Victim role. Your partner responds in Persecutor role, 'I'm sick of this, it's the same every year, let's just cancel Christmas!' Your mother, who is staying with you, joins in as Rescuer, apparently saving the day with 'It's too much for you, I'll sort it out'. Suddenly a surge of resentment means you shout at your mum, who is now in Victim (martyr) role 'I'm just trying to help!' ...and so on.*

This kind of situation plays out daily in workplaces and homes everywhere. Roles can change quickly and the outcomes are rarely positive. The drama begins when someone takes on the role of a Victim or Persecutor. They then enlist other players into the conflict, and the roles will swap and change, in a way that is often all too familiar.

To help you understand how you might use the Drama Triangle in your own life, think of a recent situation at work or home in which you found either yourself or someone else playing the 'victim' role.

It might have involved two, three or even more people in

total. Was there a Rescuer and did that rescuer become frustrated? Did any of the individuals play the part of the Persecutor? Who swapped roles during the game?

How can you step out of the triangle? It starts with awareness, so stand back and analyse your most regularly played game. If you find yourself constantly butting up against someone difficult at work or in your home life, how does it begin and what happens next? How are you feeling, and how might they be feeling?

Then think about how you could change your reaction when you find yourself in a role. If in Victim, learn to express your thoughts and feelings authentically in the moment, and ask directly for what you want and need. In other words, be more assertive. In Rescuer, help if you are asked to (and you want to) but don't take over. In Persecutor, examine your judgements about others — do they perhaps reflect things you don't like about yourself? Try showing more empathy and respect.

Again, it's about training yourself to respond in a new way.

VISUALISATION

Begin with the 'Relax and Focus Inwards' section as you did at the end of Chapter 5, i.e. finding a quiet place, using your breathing and some beautiful imagery to allow you to deepen your relaxation and drift into a feeling of comfort and well-being, then continue with this session's visualisation.

Connecting with Your Adult Self

As you allow your mind to focus inwards think of a

situation where you'd really like to be in your Adult state, feeling grounded, strong and able to think clearly. Let's begin by imagining yourself in each of the three possible states.

The first is your Parent state. Take a moment to visualise both your Critical Parent and your Nurturing Parent. Notice what you see, and what do you feel?

Next move onto your Child self. What is it like in your Child state? Are you scared or upset? Or perhaps playful, and freely expressing yourself.

Now shift into your Adult state. What does your Adult self look like... and feel like? How does your body feel? Take a few moments to really internalise that sense of confident, calm strength. Perhaps like a wise old tree, grounded, centred, strong but flexible, with firm deep roots beneath the surface to support you.

Think again about that situation where you want to be able to remain in your Adult state. Imagine how different it might be now that you can access that state so much more easily. Next time you will effortlessly know how to take yourself there.

Now gently bring yourself back to normal awareness, and back to your day, confident that you are releasing yourself from the influence of that Good Girl inside.

Chapter 10
Goodbye Good Girl!

'Whatever you can do or dream you can, begin it. Boldness has genius, power and magic in it.'
GOETHE

So now it's time to pull things together and translate what you have learnt into making some lasting changes. This means going forward with a growth mindset, breaking some rules and becoming a more brightly coloured, braver version of yourself!

You are changing your beliefs and attitudes, and starting to see yourself differently. You are actively working on self-acceptance and self-confidence, but these things alone aren't enough, because you need to begin <u>doing</u> things differently. Now I want to help you take action. Goethe said, 'Knowing is not enough; we must apply. Willing is not enough; we must do.'

Good Girls don't always know what they want. Because they are so influenced by others, they become so used to doing what their parents, friends, partners want them to do and don't ever formulate what they actually want.

So let's get down to finding, identifying and clarifying your deep-down desires. This is a perfect opportunity to really give these questions the thought they deserve:

- Is my life on course?
- What do I really want?
- What parts of my life need attention? Consider your work, family, love life, social life, hobbies, health…
- What do I want more of, or less of?
- Who might I be if my Good Girl stayed out of the way?

No more head in the sand or just making the best of things. It's so easy to get bogged down or stuck in our old patterns, but remember that we always have choices and that we have more control than we think. I'm not necessarily talking about major changes, because even a slight shift, a small change can make a huge difference. Shake things up a bit. Forget about what others think. Break some rules, break the mould! Perhaps you want to express yourself differently in the way you dress, for example. Do you have a secret desire to be more bohemian, more colourful or a little bit outrageous? No, okay that's fine — just asking!

What about how you want to spend your time? When you think about it, we don't actually spend <u>time</u>, we spend <u>life</u>. If you stay on this course, where will you be in one, two or five years? Is it where you want to be? How will you be feeling? When you grow old and look back at your life from that rocking chair, what do you want to be able to look back on? What would you like to be able to say about your life?

Whatever changes you want let's create a <u>can-do</u> attitude, focusing on what you <u>want</u>, because what you focus on you get more of. Don't wait for the perfect idea or the perfect opportunity, because it will probably never come. And no more 'I'll be happy when…'.

It's amazing how, once you get started, opportunities come along, and things begin to take shape sooner than you could have possibly imagined! Now you're going to build small stepping stones towards your goal. Don't worry if you can't see a clear route ahead. You just need to have in mind where you want to go; take the necessary action — and have faith. Sometimes I ride my bike down a cycle path near the River Thames. At certain points along the way there are barriers to negotiate — they're chicane style bars put there to prevent vehicles from using the pathway. At first, I used to stop, get off my bike and wheel it through — I was quite sure I couldn't negotiate them without falling off. But I soon realised that all I needed to do was to focus not on the obstacle, but beyond the obstacle, on the path ahead. Lo and behold, my bike and I made it through without so much as a wobble! Have faith — don't wobble, you can do it!

> *'Everything can be taken from a man but one thing: the last of the human freedoms — to choose one's attitude in any given set of circumstances — to choose one's own way.'*
> VIKTOR FRANKL, Holocaust survivor

Taking back Control

Good Girls often have an exaggerated need for control because of the fear of being vulnerable. Do you believe that having control of yourself and your personal world can protect you from life's dangers? Do you think that if you try really hard to keep on top of everything, then life will be more certain, and nothing can harm you? I doubt you will even be aware of it, but if you are at all obsessive (and many Good

Girls are), you probably subscribe to the myth that ultimate control is somehow possible. It's not.

If you tend to be anxious, the sense that you can't control things is extremely uncomfortable — and the more afraid you are the more you will want certainty. This might lead you to forget that there are many things that simply can't be controlled by you. It's very important to know the difference between what we can and can't control; it might sound obvious, but in practice it isn't at all. Even where it seems there is nothing you can do, try to take a problem-solving approach. What exactly are you worried about? Is there something you can do? There are often small ways in which you can make a difference.

I heard this idea a while back and think it's really useful. When you find yourself thinking over and over about an issue involving another person, ask yourself this: 'What's my stuff? What's their stuff? And what's God's stuff?' That way you can work out what's really within your control and help you to remember you can only control the controllables.

The Serenity Prayer
Grant me the serenity
To accept the things I cannot change
The courage to change the things I can
And wisdom to know the difference.
REINHOLD NIEBUHR

If it really is out of your hands, it's time to accept the way things are — believing that you should have been able to control it will only increase anxiety and depression. What you can do, however, is to look at the way you are interpreting it, the meaning you are making of it. Is there a more positive way of looking at it? If your job is at risk due to changes in the organisation, then yes, you can make sure you're performing as best you can, but in the end, it is probably out of your hands. It's not the end of the world. The sky will still be blue and you will survive. And who knows, it might turn out to be a blessing in disguise. Having that attitude will help you to relax and feel so much better.

The fact is we can't control everything that happens to us in life, but we can control how we respond to it.

EXERCISE: What are you tolerating?

I'd like you to take a moment to think about what you might be tolerating in your life. Naturally there will always be things or people we'd rather not have to put up with! But what might you be tolerating that you just assume you can't change. Make a list of all the things you put up with — don't make any judgement about them yet — just quickly write the list. It makes you feel quite drained just thinking about them, doesn't it! NOW decide which of those things you could do something about. Is it a question of asking someone to help? Do you need to be more honest with someone?

Stepping out of your Comfort Zone

Making changes can feel unsettling, uncomfortable or even scary. It can seem much easier to stick with the status quo; we call that 'the comfort of discomfort'. There's a wonderful poem that says it all for me:

The Comfort Zone

I used to have a comfort zone where I knew I wouldn't fail.
The same four walls and busy work, in fact more like a jail.

I longed so much to do the things I'd never done before,
But stayed inside my comfort zone and paced the same old floor.

I said it didn't matter that I wasn't doing much.
I said I didn't care for things like diamonds, furs and such.

I claimed to be so busy with things inside my zone,
But deep inside I longed for something special of my own.

I couldn't let my life go by just watching others win.
I held my breath; I stepped outside and let the change begin.

I took a step and with new strength I'd never felt before,
I kissed my comfort zone goodbye and closed and locked the door.

If you are in a comfort zone, afraid to venture out,
Remember that all winners were at one time filled with doubt.

A step or two and words of praise can make your dreams come true.
Reach for your future with a smile, success is there for you!
ANONYMOUS

Be prepared, though, because moving out of the comfort zone can sometimes cause quite hostile reactions from others. They might feel comfortable and secure when you're in that familiar zone but threatened or unhappy when you're not. It can derail your efforts to move forward if you are not ready for it.

There's an argument that says if you're growing as an individual, you're always going to be out of your comfort zone. And if you're worried about making changes, have courage — although it feels uncomfortable to begin with, you can cope with that feeling because the benefits outweigh the discomfort. Embrace it.

Making Decisions

Bearing in mind Good Girls worry about what others think, about breaking rules and making mistakes, it's no wonder that decision-making may feel like a very risky business.

For every one of us life is a journey, full of ups and downs, twists and turns. It is your challenging experiences that teach you more about yourself and the world. They increase self-awareness and open you up to true personal growth. Good Girls often spend too much time trying to make the 'right' decision and sometimes if the anxiety becomes too intense, they will avoid making any decisions at all, and even the minor daily ones become a trial.

Instead they accept the status quo and miss opportunities to make progress in life. Being indecisive, holding onto your options, doubting, avoiding commitment can be expensive — in terms of time, energy spent, lost opportunities. There's a lot of truth in the old adage 'Not to decide *is* to decide — and often for the worse'.

> '*Life shrinks or expands in proportion to your courage.*' ANAÏS NIN

165

We've all heard people say 'I'm in a no-win situation'. But keep in mind that whatever you choose doesn't need to define the rest of your life, and *every* choice has benefits to offer you. Instead, try to think of each choice in terms of 'no lose'; after all, you never <u>really</u> know what would have happened if you'd taken another path? And to be honest, how often are the consequences of a decision catastrophic?

Stand back and focus on being more accepting and pleased with any positive outcomes from your decisions. As long as you remain overwhelmingly concerned about a negative outcome, you'll be afraid to make a decision. On the other hand, if you can be okay with whatever happens, you'll be much more able to choose a path. Approaching things this way allows for complete freedom of choice without thinking in terms of failure.

Of course, you will want to consider all the options when making important decisions, but <u>then</u> you need to connect with your 'gut feeling'. We all feel a certain amount of apprehension about change, but if you connect with your most visceral feelings, you'll know what feels right.

So if you're considering taking a new job, leaving a dysfunctional relationship or moving house, but are feeling very torn, how do you know if it's simply apprehension or feels fundamentally wrong? I usually find that apprehension will involve lots of mental activity — going over options, worrying about how things will be, maybe focusing on the difficulties of settling in. If something is just wrong for me, this is a much more physical feeling, a heavy, unpleasant feeling in my 'gut'. If I'm feeling this, then all the thinking in the world won't make it feel right!

Then once you've made your decision, take a breath and don't look back! What makes a decision good or bad largely depends on what you tell yourself after you've made it.

What Might Hold You Back?

> '*Twenty years from now you will be more disappointed by the things you didn't do than by the ones you did do.*
> *So throw off the bowlines. Sail away from the safe harbour. Catch the trade winds in your sails. Explore. Dream. Discover.*'
> H. JACKSON BROWN JNR

Have a think now about what obstacles there might be to making these changes. You may need to learn to get out of your own way. Obstacles can be real but we forget that they can also be imagined. In other words, are they the product of your negative thinking or self-limiting beliefs? What do you think is your No 1 obstacle? Fear of failure? Guilt? Lack of confidence? Lack of motivation? Lack of energy? Lack of money? Lack of time? Worry about what others might say? About upsetting someone? Be honest.

Amongst the most common is **fear of failure.** But the truth is if you don't fail sometimes, then you aren't really living your life. Successful people don't give up; instead, they learn resilience through their trials and tribulations. They don't look back — they look forward. All successful people will fail, often many times! Thomas Edison, the inventor whose work led to the creation of the electric light bulb, found 10,000 ways that <u>didn't</u> work before he succeeded. You could say failure is the foundation of success; indeed, evidence is all around you. There are so many successful people in society — politicians, CEOs, celebrities — who have made major mistakes, fallen from grace and risen again. I rest my case.

- Think back to a time when you failed at something. Take a moment to reflect on what learning you might take from that experience.
- What would it mean if you did fail? What positive learning could you take from it in the future?

Don't be one of those people who say 'I never try anything I won't be good at!' Instead make a point of trying new things just for the hell of it and with no expectations at all.

When your Good Girl adopts her cautious persona, check that her reluctance is unfounded. Then send her into the background and hold fast to the plan.

> *'The greatest glory in living lies not in never falling, but in rising every time we fall.'*
> NELSON MANDELA

What about **guilt**? If you've spent a lot of your time in the past pleasing other people and not taking care of yourself, you may feel unfulfilled yet uncomfortably guilty at the thought of considering your own needs! Do those around you discourage you in your endeavours? They may be jealous, think it will take too much of your time, energy, or simply not understand how important this is to you. Remember this is for YOU. Give yourself permission to put your own needs first.

It's about giving yourself permission. Your Good Girl has

been responsible for a lot of hesitation and things need to change.

If you have trouble getting **motivated**, give yourself a good talking to! Remind yourself why you want this — what it will mean to you. Why do you need the change — what difference will it make? Imagine if you don't do it. How will you feel in in a few years' time when nothing has changed? Renew your focus, do whatever it takes to get your energy level up.

EXERCISE: What energises you? What drains You?

We're all different, so the things that recharge my batteries will not do the same for you. Take a sheet of paper and make two columns, one headed 'Energises', the other headed 'Drains'. This exercise is similar to the Tolerations one earlier in this chapter. First just do a brain dump on each column — anything, however small, can go on the list — make no judgement. It could be walking in the rain, playing loud rock music, or growing orchids (a recent passion of mine) that energises you. Doing the supermarket shopping, calling your sister or struggling with a slow computer might drain you.

The idea is to see if you can include more pleasurable, energising activities in your life, and reduce the impact of those that drain you. Several years ago, I realised that I really hate doing the food shopping. I seem to have been doing it forever — well, it <u>has</u> been for some decades! I happen to know that my other half hates many of the household duties (ask me how I know), but he loves his food. He was perfectly happy to do the supermarket shopping. Then I decided to lighten my load even further by getting a cleaner once a fortnight — worth every penny. Result! I don't know why I didn't do it earlier. It certainly removed one obstacle to writing this book.

Now for each obstacle — ask: 'Is this within my control?' It's about taking responsibility for your own life. It's no good blaming our circumstances, our childhood or our partner when we find life is passing us by. It may not be a major change — but if it would make a difference to you, then it's worth the effort. A great question to ask yourself for each obstacle is: 'What might I be assuming here?'

The Russian Olympic competitor Vasily Alexeev was trying to break a weightlifting record of 500 lbs. He had lifted 499 but couldn't lift 500 however hard he tried. Finally, his trainers put 501.5 lbs on his bar and rigged it so it looked like 499 lbs. Of course, you know what happened; he lifted it easily. Once he created this new reality other weightlifters went on to break his record. Why? Because they knew it was possible to lift 500 lbs.

The limits we set for ourselves exist in our minds. If we go with our hearts, believe in ourselves, we can dissolve the barriers. Why shouldn't you? You deserve to have the best life you can!

Staying on Track

How are you spending your time? Remember that time itself may be infinite but your time is finite, and how you spend your days is how you spend your life. In the past your Good Girl has probably led you to spend a lot of time doing what others want, holding back from following your own course, and dancing to a different tune from one you would choose for yourself. So now that you have decided things will change it's important to hold yourself to account. Regularly review how you're spending your time, and who you're spending it with. Look at how well you're practising self-care. Adjust accordingly. This is your life to spend in the way that works for you.

Mindful Living (Enjoying the journey)

Most of our time is spent either thinking about the future or the past, and we forget to enjoy the moments that make up the journey. Yesterday is gone and tomorrow has yet to arrive. This moment is the only one that is real. So resolve to take time to appreciate more the simple things in life...enjoy the changing seasons, the smell of hot coffee, snuggling down in a warm bed.

Take pleasure from those things that appeal to the senses. Tune in to the wonders around you. As I sit here now in my little summerhouse (or shed!), I glance out of the window and notice the sweetest little blue tit sitting on the wall watching me. I find myself smiling — a moment of joy. I even convince myself we have a fleeting connection, as two creatures just getting on with life.

> 'Yesterday is history. Tomorrow is a mystery. Today is a gift. That is why it is called the present.'
> ALICE MORSE EARLE

We are not machines and yet much of modern life feels like being on a constantly moving treadmill. Be grateful for being alive, because that feeling of gratitude (irrespective of whether you are religious or not) is a joyful feeling and... good feelings bring <u>more</u> good feelings!

Mindfulness practice is a very simple form of meditation that was little known in the West until fairly recently. Although there are various approaches, it's not a religion, it's not complicated and doesn't need take long. It's a kind of mental training if you like, and you can practise it anywhere. It's about befriending things as they are. Typically, it involves focusing your full attention on your breath as it flows in and out of your body, observing your thoughts as they arise and, making no judgement, and little by little letting go of your struggle with them.

You can watch thoughts as they appear in your mind, seemingly from thin air, and watch again as they disappear, and you come to realise that they come and go of their own accord. They are not who you are, or even part of who you are. You will begin to truly understand that thoughts and feelings (including negative ones) are transient. They come and go, and you have a choice about whether to make meaning from them, act on them or simply do nothing.

Jon Kabat-Zinn describes mindfulness as 'dropping in on ourselves', feeling how it is to be in *this* mind, in *this* body in *this* moment.

We're constantly creating stories about ourselves, making meaning out of things (often getting it wrong), grasping for outcomes. Yet it's exactly the kind of mind that gets in the way of the outcome, for example, if you tell yourself how vitally important that meeting is tomorrow, it leads to 'what ifs', then another thought and another...

Mindfulness is about observing without criticising; being kind and compassionate to yourself. When you feel overwhelmed with negative thoughts you learn not to take things personally, to simply observe them as they pass.

Imagine this as watching traffic on a busy road. You merely sit at the side of the road observing, sometimes curious, sometimes less interested. You don't get out there *in with* the traffic! Essentially, mindfulness allows you to catch negative thought patterns before they send you into a downward spiral. You can begin to take back control in this way. There's lots of information out there on mindfulness. I love Ruby Wax's book *A Mindfulness Guide for the Frazzled*. It's practical, witty and very accessible. If you'd like to try a progressive mindfulness course, check out the app from www.headspace.com.

Mindfulness Exercise

1. Sit quietly. Close your eyes. You're going to notice what's happening moment by moment, living your life as if it matters, moment by moment, able to participate in your own well-being. No striving, just being. Open up to every moment as a new beginning… paying attention. Step outside time. Let it all go for the moment. Let it be as it is… not wishing or hoping.

2. Take a few deep, abdominal breaths (imagine a balloon expanding in abdomen as you breathe in). Cool in, warm out. Letting go… feel yourself flow into the space around you.

3. Then allow your breathing to be natural. If you like, you can count the rise and fall of the breath. Become aware of gravity, of physical sensations. Scan your body — bring it into your awareness. Notice how you feel, your mood, your level of relaxation. Notice sounds and smells. Allow your body to 'soften and flow'.

4. Observe thoughts as they come and go — no control needed.

5. Now let go of any focus… all is well.

6. Then bring back attention to your body.

7. Come back into normal awareness.

Research has shown that meditation of all kinds helps prevent depression, positively affects mood and the brain patterns underlying day-to-day anxiety. Other studies show that clarity of thinking, memory and creativity improve. Gradually it creates a feeling of greater well-being and happiness. What's more, research shows that regular meditators see their doctors less often and spend fewer days in hospital.

Keeping a Journal

Regular reflection (as opposed to self-absorption) is a great habit to get into, and writing down your thoughts and observations is even more beneficial. A journal provides a space where you can hold a thoughtful, honest conversation with yourself, slowing down those vague, chaotic thoughts, giving them structure and bringing some clarity. You can look back and see how far you've come, or when you're having a bad day, remind yourself that there are plenty of good days too.

People have been writing down their thoughts, experiences, hopes and dreams for centuries, but research over the last twenty years has produced strong evidence for its many benefits, so it is often seen as an integral part of therapy and coaching. Not only does it improve emotional wellbeing and make you happier, it boosts immunity, can reduce blood pressure and even enhance sporting performance. We know that denying our feelings can lead to long-term stress and disease, and journaling is a way of acknowledging emotions, increasing self-awareness and perhaps asking, 'Why did I do that?' or 'What was really going on there?'

Your journal will become like a friend who's always there. It's a special place where you can make sense of life, so it's important to set some quiet time aside. Whether five minutes or 20 minutes the key is to make it manageable and realistic. There are no rules, except to be as honest with yourself as possible! No need to include everything, it's not a masterpiece and doesn't have to be perfect. Make it something you look forward to, definitely NOT another 'must do'!

Perhaps you'll hand write it in a special notebook. Advances in neuroscience and brain imaging have led to the discovery that writing by hand, as opposed to typing, activates parts of the brain that help us to think, producing greater activity in areas on both sides of the brain. But the important thing is to actually do it, so if you prefer to use your computer or phone, that's fine too. There are plenty of journal templates online if you like that idea.

It will take practice if you aren't used to being introspective, and it's a new habit that will need to become established. But stick with it for a month, and you'll be surprised at the results!

Review Your Progress

It's one thing making plans for change, but it's easy to lose focus when the day-to-day stuff gets in the way. Create an action plan to keep you on track, to help remind you of what you want, how you plan to get there and how far you've come! It won't be a smooth road from Good Girl to throwing the rule book away, because all personal change takes time and effort. So even if it's three steps forward and two steps back sometimes, provided you're headed in the right direction, that's progress.

Your Good Girl will always be part of you, and so she should be — we need our old scars to remind us we've lived! But it will be worth all the effort, as you slowly experience a sense of lightness and freedom. The freedom to be fully yourself.

> *'Trust yourself. Create the kind of self that you will be happy to live with all your life. Make the most of yourself by fanning the tiny, inner sparks of possibility into flames of achievement.'*
> GOLDA MEIR

VISUALISATION

Begin with the 'Relax and Focus Inwards' section as you did at the end of Chapter 5, i.e. finding a quiet place, using your breathing and some beautiful imagery to allow you to deepen your relaxation and drift into a feeling of comfort and wellbeing, then continue with this session's visualisation.

Creating a compelling future

Now, it's time for you to create your future, the way you want it to be. You're really beginning to grow into your true self now. Breaking some rules, caring less about what others think and beginning to see yourself differently. More and more you find yourself focusing on what you want and not what you don't want, and you are allowing yourself to dream of new freedoms, of a feeling of liberation. And you know that whatever you want, you can begin to move towards it with a more positive mindset, accepting that it might be uncomfortable at times but having the courage to know it's right for you. You are enjoying the freedom to flourish as yourself, no longer held back by those Good Girl ideas.

176

You begin to see yourself in the future where you have discarded those outdated negative messages about yourself and moved beyond past hurts and disappointment. You feel a sense of joy as you realise you are no longer afraid to try new things.

Now think of an event or occasion in the future and see yourself having moved forward into that time, into the future you want. What are you doing? Where are you and who's there with you? Visualise the colours, the details, the sounds, and feel a sense of pride and achievement. Notice that sense of wellbeing and happiness that comes from achieving desired change. Think of the obstacles you overcame, and feel so happy as you remember you overcame them all; setbacks were only blips in your progress. You have proved to yourself that you have the courage to do whatever it takes, one step at a time.

Keep that future self in your mind, visit your future often and each time you do you will strengthen your ability to make it real. Now you're really enjoying the journey towards becoming your true self!

Gently bring yourself back to normal awareness, and back to your day, confident that you are releasing yourself from the influence of that Good Girl inside.

A FINAL WORD

I hope this book has inspired you to make those changes and fulfil your potential. Progress might seem slow at times but be patient — although personal change takes time, the benefits are most definitely there for you.

I promised you a 'how to' book, so make the most of the many tools and techniques in these pages. Make lots of notes and keep this book where you can easily find it when you need it.

You now know how you've been feeding your Good Girl and how you can reduce her influence in your life. You know how to be compassionate to yourself and embrace your authentic self. You have the tools to communicate better — to ask for what you want and to say what you think. And you have learnt to keep your emotions in check as you do all that. If you choose it, this is the beginning of a journey into a compelling future.

I wish you the very best of everything.

Getting support

If you are feeling overwhelmed by stress, anxiety or feel your mental health is suffering, please consider seeing a therapist. Having someone to talk to, someone who is non-judgemental and there just for you, can make a massive difference. Talking about problems gives them structure and gets them out where you can see them. It will help you to feel as if you've taken back some control and set you on a much more positive path.

Resources

Rewire your Anxious Brain by Catherine M. Pittman PhD, Elizabeth M. Karle MLIS. New Harbinger

Non-violent Communication: A Language of Life by Marshall B. Rosenberg. Puddledancer Press

The Endorphin Effect by William Bloom. Piatkus

Daring Greatly by Brené Brown. Penguin Life

Overcoming Perfectionism by Jenny Gould. www.bookboon.com

Managing Anxiety at Work by Jenny Gould.www.bookboon.com

Cognitive Therapy of Depression by Aaron T. Beck. The Guilford Press

New Ways of Seeing: The Art of Therapeutic Reframing by Mark Tyrell. Uncommon Knowledge

Making Up the Mind: How the Brain Creates our Mental World by Chris Firth. Blackwell Publishing

Emotional Intelligence by Daniel Goleman. Bloomsbury Publishing

TA Today: A New Introduction to Transactional Analysis by Ian Stewart and Vann Joines. Lifespace Publishing

Perfectionism: Theory, Research and Treatment by Gordon L. Flett, Paul L. Hewitt, 2002, American Psychological Association

When Perfect Isn't Good Enough by Martin M. Antony, PH.D.

and Richard P. Swinson, MD. 2009, New Harbinger Publications, Inc.

Overcoming Perfectionism: The Key to a Balanced Recovery by Ann W. Smith M.S., 1990, Health Communications Inc.

Too Perfect: When Being in Control Gets Out of Control by Allan E. Mallinger, M.D., Jeannette De Wyze 1992, Clarkson Potter Publishers.

Women Who Love Too Much by Robin Norwood. Arrow

Bravely You, Bravely Me: *Being You Without Apology* by Chiron O'Keefe

Lost Connections by Johann Hari. Bloomsbury Publishing

The Women's Brain by Dr Sarah McKay. Hachette Australia

The Nice Girl Syndrome by Beverly Engel. Wiley

Emotional Agility: Get Unstuck, Embrace Change and Thrive in Work and Life by Susan David. Penguin

Reinventing Your Life: Jeffrey E. Young. Penguin Putnam

Emotional Child Abuse: The Family Curse by Joel Covitz. Sigo Press U.S.

A Mindfulness Guide for the Frazzled: Ruby Wax. Penguin Life

Healing the Shame That Binds You by John Bradshaw. HCI Books

Human Givens Institute

A Short Course in Happiness After Loss: (And Other Dark, Difficult Times) by Maria Sirois

Overcoming Perfectionism by Jenny Gould. Bookboon.com

Managing Anxiety at Work by Jenny Gould. Bookboon.com